Hope, Life, and Inspiration
A Collection of Poetry and Prose

by
Jim Cox

Text copyright 2015 by James Delar Cox. All rights reserved. All of the poems and stories in this work are original and do not infringe upon the legal rights of any other person or work. No part of this book may be reproduced or transmitted in any form or by any means, electronic or mechanical, including photography, recording, or any information storage and retrieval system, without permission in writing from the publisher. The only exceptions are brief excerpts and reviews.

Author: Jim Cox
Editor: Lynn Bemer Coble
Book and Cover Designer: Jennifer Tipton Cappoen

1589 Skeet Club Road, Suite 102-175
High Point, NC 27265
www.PawsandClawsPublishing.com
info@pawsandclawspublishing.com

ISBN #978-0-99060607-7-2
Printed in the United States

Acknowledgements

I am overjoyed that all of the proceeds from my book will help to support the Organ and Endowment Funds at Christ Lutheran Church in Greensboro, North Carolina.

Bless all of you for taking my words and putting them into this precious book, but especially for making my dream a reality. I'm sending a very special thanks to those on the Poetry Book Committee at Christ Lutheran who took on the task of creating this book and worked diligently on it. For editing, typing, collating, organizing, and categorizing my poems and stories, thanks goes out to all of the following: Carol Alala, Jean Apple, Pat Best, Maggie Bull, Genny Cobrda, Linda Deese, Patryck Nuss, Jane Readling, Nancy Shellaway, and Beth Woodard.

Thank you also to Martin Enriquez for taking photographs of the reredos (carved Christ figure) and baptismal window at Christ Lutheran to use for the book's covers.

Jim Cox

Dedication

This book is dedicated to all the members of Christ Lutheran Church in Greensboro, North Carolina, over the past 25 years in honor of all the love they gave my family and me during this past time. Without this love, I could not have made it.

I have married two angels in my life, Ethel and Shirley. I enjoy spending time with my seven daughters: Carollyn, Donna, Becky, Melissa, Melanie, Rachel, and Roberta; fifteen grandchildren; and seventeen great grandchildren.

I dedicate this book to the glory of God. I love to share my faith and love of God with others, especially on a one-on-one basis.

Jim Cox

Table of Contents

Church	9
Evangelism	21
Faith	31
Family and Special People	51
Giving Thanks	63
Heaven and Angels	67
Love	73
Prayer	89
Professions	93
Questioning	99
Reflections	111
Salvation	121
Seasons	131
Christmas	132
New Year	147
Lent	149
Easter	154
Special Times	162
Sympathy	165
Trust	173
STORIES OF INSPIRATION	185
About the Author	226

Church

Baptism

Jesus went down to the Jordan for John to wash His sins away.
God from the heavens proclaimed His son that joyous day.

With the baptismal water, we are all made members of
    God's family to stay.
But we must keep the relationship daily by talking to Him
    when we pray.
The water washes away the sins we must watch for every day.
When they sneak upon us all, we have to take them to Him
    when we pray.

Each time we see water, we should remember the vows
    that were said
And the awful price our Savior had to pay hanging on
    the cross until He was dead.

Baptism is free, but it must be lived every day.
We should give Him thanks with every prayer that we say.

The Lord's Table

Come to His table and eat.
What you receive will be the greatest treat.

Come to His table and drink.
It will do you more good than you think.

Come to His table and pray,
For His forgiveness is the only way.

Come to His table with your brothers,
For He will treat you as He does all the others.

Come to His table at every chance and receive.
All the forgiveness you get you will never perceive.

This is His body. This is His blood.
It will protect you from the sinful flood.

The meal you received is freely given.
It will last you until you get to heaven.

Go and Serve

You are serving the Lord when you are singing in the choir.
You are serving the Lord when you stop and visit another member for an hour.
You are serving the Lord when you bake a cake and take it to a friend.
You are serving the Lord just sitting with a dying friend to the end.
You are serving the Lord when you tell them about God's power.
You are serving the Lord when you tell of His love, even in a gentle shower.
You are serving the Lord when you read to someone who has no sight.
You are serving the Lord when you greet everyone with a smile so bright.
You are serving the Lord when you feed someone in a homeless shelter.
You are serving the Lord when you point out to someone the beauty of a river delta.
Know the Lord is with you in each task you may do.
Remember to His love always be true.

Our Pastor

We knew you were the one when you walked down the aisle
    of the church.
We knew you were God's answer to our very long search.

Oh what a deal we got when we extended you the call.
We got Nancy also and she keeps you on the ball.

There have been many tears that have been shed.
But with your leadership, you have kept us looking ahead.

The knowledge of God's word you have helped us to see.
The peace you have taught us has set our souls free.

This is to tell you how much we love and appreciate all
    that you do.
Whatever we face in the future, we will trust you to see
    us through.

Nine Years Ago

Can you believe nine years ago they joined our little flock?

It's passed so quickly like a few ticks of the clock.

Oh what a deal we got when we extended that call,

Not knowing what Pastor and Nancy had on the ball.

If it is God's word you want to hear,

He will tell you like it is without any fear.

A more-devoted couple we never could have found,

No matter where we looked in city or town.

Thank you both for these nine years of your time.

Let's hope God will keep you with us for a long, long time.

Church

Eleven Years of Love

It's been eleven years since Pastor and Nancy joined
    our group.
We have had many meals together. Everything from
    communion to soup.

Always willingly our burdens they have faithfully shared.
In times of sorrow, they have been there to say that they cared.

Over the years their love for God and each other they
    have shown to all.
Each day we should thank God that they answered our call.

His knowledge of the Bible has taught us a lot.
We all dearly love this wonderful couple that we got.

Looking for a Dozen More

Twelve years ago Pastor and Nancy came to live here.
As the years have passed, we have learned to hold them dear.
Their witness of love has taught us about true devotion.
Their love can only be exceeded by Christ's resurrection.

They have been by our side in sadness and in our joys.
Through Pastor's teachings we have learned God's love is real
    and not some ploy.
To stress the point of some messages, he has played many
    different roles,
All to make sure we commit to God our heart and souls.

Cookies, donuts, and roses these days are being sold by
    the dozen,
So Pastor and Nancy we hope and pray you are ready to start
    your second dozen.
Words cannot express the love we feel for you so deep in
    our hearts.
It has grown deeper year by year from the very start.

Church

Thirty-five and Ten

Thirty-five years ago he was ordained and sent on his way.
He was told to go teach people how to live, love, and pray.
Ten years ago he came to lead our little church.
This was the answer to a very long and hard search.

His thirty-five years of service have sent him far and wide.
But he will go anywhere with his faithful bride at his side.
When we placed the call, we felt he was sent from God above.
Over the years this wonderful pair we have come to love.

Through the ups and downs, they have passed the hardest test.
Proving once again that God always knows the very best.
Let us once again say, "Pastor and Nancy, we love you truly
And praise God that He has led you both to His work so holy."

It's Been Fifty

Fifty years ago this very day, a group gathered to pray.
They asked for God's guidance as they started on their way.
A leader was chosen and he started them thinking about
    God's will.
He taught them to look for God's direction on where
    they should build.

The church was built with much prayer, love, and care.
People came to do God's work from almost everywhere.
They scrubbed, they sewed, they mopped. All wanting to do
    their share
Because they knew that in this house, God would always
    be there.

Some of the pastors were meek, and some were very bold.
Their cause the same: bringing souls into God's fold.
Out of the children who came from this little flock,
We can claim pastors, lawyers, teachers, and even a doc.

What love members had for each soul that was gathered to
    the flock.
Their love was so contagious that it spread over every block.
As all of them gathered to spread the work of the Lord,
Some grew in faith while others dropped out because they
    were bored.

Church

There were many who came to help spread God's will,
But it was the Holy Spirit who would not let them sit still.
It's God who calls us all to accept His everlasting love.
By accepting this love, we are assured a place in heaven above.

Let's give thanks to all whom God has led to join us as we pray
And pray He will continue to lead others our way.
Joy is found every time we stop to pray.
Let us give thanks to all who have paved the way.

What's Love?

Love is found in every church member.
This love runs deep even into the church's every timber.

It is what covers you with cards when you are ill.
It is what brings you food to make sure you have your fill.

This love helps us to feed those who are hungry and poor.
It helps us to heal the weary and those who are sore.

You may visit other groups who meet for one reason or another.
But nowhere will you find this love that makes you feel like a
    sister or brother.

God's love is found this whole world so wide.
But in church He sits in your pew on either side.

Love can be found at home or almost anywhere.
But the love you find here, you will know we really care.

Whether you are weary or tired or just in need of prayer,
Come sit in a pew and this love you will really share.

Evangelism

Feed My Sheep

Have you fed Christ's word to someone today?
Even when life is so busy, try to tell anyone you meet along
    the way
The story of God's blessed love.
This was one of Christ's wishes before He went to His
    home above.

Reach out and tell someone what He has done for you.
Tell them about your faith and what it means to you.
You do not need to fill them with food or drink.
Just share His love and tell them what you think.

We are all Christ's herd, wherever we may roam.
But we must spread Christ's message before we go home.

Find Peace and Share It

We all talk about peace, but most people never find it.
Some write songs about peace, but most are not big hits.

Peace is what everyone should be seeking the most
But can only be found when it is given us by the Holy Ghost.

Peace usually comes after lives are lost in many major battles.
But it is as fragile as a light bulb put in a bag and shaken till
    it rattles.

True peace can only last when it is put in each heart by our
    Lord and Savior.
You can know this peace, and others can tell it by your
    behavior.

Peace must be in every heart, or it will not last very long.
But when peace fills every heart, life is like a beautiful song.

Accept that love and pass it on to others.
This peace will make us treat all as sisters and brothers.

He Was Like Us

He was born, He lived, He died, and He returned.
By believing this, our eternity has been earned.

Now we must share our faith in Him with others,
For He taught us that all are our sisters and brothers.

Have you thanked Him for these blessings today?
Take time to be His witness as you go on your way.

Our life here is not long, so many have said.
But we strive to help others in the way He has led.

Your faith and trust are shown in your actions to others.
So greet those you meet with a love as tender as your mother's.

He paid the price when He died for us all.
Spread it to others so they too may answer His call.

Pass It On

Never pass up a chance to tell what Christ did for you.
He has given you eternal life by your faith. You know
    it is true.
He gave you life and led you to those who love you
    so much.
He gave you love, hope, and faith that you spread to all
    whom you touch.

He gave you air to breathe, water to drink, and a brain
    to think.
He gave you birds of all sizes and flowers of all colors,
    like yellow and pink.
You use these things He has given you and know they will
    be there without a doubt.
Tell all you meet about His love and your faith, plant a
    seed, and pray it will sprout.

You know God is everywhere, so share it with all both
    day and night.
By passing it on, someday we will all get to live
    in His light.

Reach Out

Reach out and touch someone today.
You will never know what it will take to make them okay.
Each miracle has to start in a tiny way.
It could be an act or a word you have to say.

Many lives are changed when you stop to pray.
You should always take your thoughts to the Lord
    without delay.
Prayer is so handy. And God's never too busy to care.
He says, "Call me and I will always be there."

He hears each prayer said silent or aloud.
He hears them if you are alone or in a crowd.

God's love is for all the sick or the able,
So you should pray at the altar or the table.
You should thank Him as often as you can
And try to live by His everlasting plan.

The things you do sometimes speak louder than the words,
And the results that come may never be heard.
Reach out and tell others what God's love does for you
And that your faith in His word will always be true.

Share His Love

We have experienced the joy of Christ's rebirth.
We know what He has planned for His followers
     here on earth.

The time has come for us to share our faith every day.
Never pass up a chance to tell it along the way.

God's blessings are seen with every step you take.
Point them out to people for their own sake.

A joyous life is promised to all who believe His word.
Just believe and see His love in every word
     you have heard.

Tell everyone of the joy that Christ has given to you.
That His salvation was for all, not just a chosen few.

Tell everyone we are known as His Easter people.
Let them know that is why there is a cross on our steeple.

Tell them we too will overcome death as He did
By believing and serving others at His bid.

What He has said is a blessing in every way.
Be sure you tell of His life and love every day.

Sharing

Have you shared God's love with someone today?
Have you helped someone enjoy a special day?
The sharing of God's love is the most blessed gift to give.
It will tell everyone just what makes you live.
Sharing God's love will bring you a great delight.
It encourages those whom you meet to do everything right.

Sharing your faith will only make it grow stronger.
It will shorten a path that with each day seems
    to grow longer.
Share with each other your faith in your Savior above.
Tell everyone that God's gift of His son was to show
    His love.

Sharing the truth is a joy sent from above.
Tell everyone about the delight of His caring and love.
Let us tell of His love as we have been told.
Let us tell everyone that His love will keep us in the fold.

The Reason

Love is the reason we are here on earth.
It was given to you by God at your birth.

You must spread it to others, everywhere you go.
Love will always ease the way wherever your life will flow.
Sometimes it's hard to understand where love is going.
But—wherever it takes you—God's love is not boring.
Love led Christ to the cross, but He made the choice.
That love will help you. Just listen to His voice.

Sometimes God's love is hard for us to understand.
But we must remember His ways are greater than
     mortal man's.
Sometimes the way is hard to face, but He is always there.
No matter what, it is His love that will say I do care.

God's love is more powerful than anything on earth,
And Christ paid the price to show what it is worth.

Using Time for God

How many times have you heard someone say,
"My time is mine, and I do as I please"?
Every moment we have is a gift from God, and
It should be spent for Him with love and ease.

He gave us this time to help each other,
But it is spent for our own pleasure.
It's good to enjoy life, but God should
Also get an equal measure.

We can use His time every day by telling someone
And helping them to understand
His love is for all, both rich and poor.
It doesn't matter if we are woman or man.

Our days here are limited. Some get a lot and some
    only a few.
His blessings are spread to all equally, just like drops
    of morning dew.

When you awake each morning, go to Him for His plans
    for your day.
Then start out with Him. Get His words spread to all
    you meet along the way.

Faith

Always There

When you get tired and weary, it's to the Lord you can turn.
When you have strayed from His ways, you know it's to Him
    you can return.

When the burdens get so heavy, you know He will help with
    the task.
When the world seems to be after you, you can hold
    to Him fast.

When you are showered with blessings, be sure to give
    Him praise.
For it is His will that the sun will set and that the sun will raise.

When the heavens open up and the rains start to fall,
It may be a curse for some, but it could be a blessing
    for them all.

When you wake in the morning and the weather is just right,
Give thanks to the Lord for such a wonderful sight.

When temptations try to lead you from the proven way,
Remember that He has said, "I will forgive you when you stray."

Faith

Don't Wait

When was the last time you shared what your faith means
 to you?
When was the last time you said to someone, "I love you"?
When was the last time you stopped and told God,
 "Thank you"?
When was the last time you looked up at the sky so blue?
When did you last thank God for what His son did for you?
When did you call a friend and ask, "Is there anything I can
 do for you?"

Life is busy, and your time is spread out so thin.
You must slow down and tell others how Christ died for
 your every sin.

Never wait for tomorrow to share your thoughts. Do it today.
You are not promised tomorrow. You must show God's love
 each day.

Faith for Sure

When your spirits are down, there is one place to go.
Down on your knees talking to the Lord, for He told you so.

When you are feeling great and full of glee, this is where
    you should be,
Thanking Him for taking your worries and setting you free.

He said, "Come to me, you who are laden. And I will
    give you rest."
Put your faith and trust in Him, for His actions are best.

Sometimes when my spirit is low and I'm full of doubt,
I get on my knees and talk. Then I know what His plan
    is all about.

Faith, hope, and love will make the hardest life
    a glorious dream.
Remember to hold on tight to your faith,
    and the Lord will keep you on the beam.

Faith

Focus Right

Be sure to always focus on the cross.
You will always have a gain. There will be no loss.
From early times the North Star was always there.
Likewise, put your faith in God for your every care.

The early sailors had to be sure their aim was right.
We must make sure the love on the cross is in sight.
God set the path, and Jesus showed us the way.
Turn to Them for your guidance as you live each day.

Take your eyes from the cross and you will go astray.
You will meet many evils on your way each day.

Like the star in the sky led Wise Men in their day,
Our faith in God in heaven will lead us on our way.
People have changed and depend on other things
    to guide their way,
But we must pray and trust God to lead us each day.

Our focus must always be where it got its start.
On that cross where our God poured love from His heart.
The sailors of old knew the North Star was always there.
We know God's love can reach us anywhere.

God Can Change Anything

You can look around and see His changes everywhere you look.
He can change a raging stream into a gently flowing brook.

He can change a violently erupting volcano of red-hot lava
Into a serene mountainside that grows beans to make java.

He can change a wind-driven storm of hard-falling rain
Into a gentle little shower to nourish a flowerbed or
    fields of grain.

He can change the roughest people—both young and old—
Into kind, loving people by reaching into their souls.

Nothing is impossible for God to reach out and change.
Through prayer and faith, everything is in His loving range.

He can change a beach mired by towering waves
Into a place where everyone can relax and enjoy His sun's rays.

God's Internet

Are you connected to God's Internet of trust, faith, and love?
Sign on and start spreading the word about God's heavenly
    home above.
A place we all search for most of the time we are here
    on God's earth.
His Internet has no disconnect. We are on it from
    our earthly birth.

His Facebook is open. And in it He can find anything you do.
He knows each sin as well as each act of love we do to be true.

God's Internet is spread wide from pole to pole
    all over the place.
He is connected to every country, and His love is for
    every race.

Sign on today, put the volume on high, and tell everyone
    they will need Him by and by.
Because without that connection, we will never reach
    that home in the sky.

Growing in Faith

When I was young, I went to Sunday school
Where I learned all about the Golden Rule.
What I was taught at an early age
Has served me as an aid in living life's every page.

A solid foundation is needed to build a strong belief.
Through good times and bad times, your faith
    will bring you relief.
A faith in God will never let you down.
He will always give you a smile, never a frown.

Faith

Keep Your Eyes on the Lord

Over the side Peter stepped without fear,
Because His Master had told him to come near.
But when Peter took his eyes off Him,
He realized he was lost because he could not swim.

Christ calls us to follow in His way,
Because He knows we are likely to stray.
If we follow Him and do what He has said,
He will lead and love us. He will make sure His sheep are fed.

Keep your eyes upon the Savior and follow in His ways.
He will give you peace of mind each and every day.
When things get too hard to carry, take them to Him
    in prayer.
He will help you over them and make sure you get there.

His arms are always open, no matter where we've been.
It's our faith and trust that will see us through to the end.

Lead Us

Jesus, Savior of our souls, take our hands and lead us home.
With your love you can soften a soul as hard as stone.

Jesus, Savior, You can show us the way.
But stay close by to pull us back if we start to stray.

We are tempted in so many ways,
But enable us to always give You the praise.

Jesus, Savior, You have again made us whole.
Lead us to reach to others to bring them to the fold.

Jesus, Savior, You are the spark that can light the way.
Lead us to use that light to brighten someone else's day.

Jesus, Savior, You know the price You paid
To be able to bring all of us back to the path You laid.

Faith

Let Me See

Jesus, open my eyes that I might see,
As you did for the blind man in answer to his plea.
Give me the faith that he had so long ago
To go out and tell how You loved me so.
Though I wasn't blind from birth like he,
There are so many things you want me to see.
I am blind to some of the needs of my fellowman.
With Your help, his problems I can understand.

He went to the lake as he was told;
Jesus, give me the strength to be so bold.
I go down the road and see the things You want me to see,
But I am still blind to realize how things should be.
Open my eyes that I may see the goodness to be found in others.
Let me learn Your will to live as if we were all brothers.
Lord, I am often blind to the things that I should see.
Sometimes I forget that You died on that cross to set me free.

Lord, it is my fervent prayer that each and every day,
You will reach down and keep us all from going astray.

Lift Your Cross

You must say to yourself, "No matter this weight,
    I will carry the cross,
Because the Lord is with me and He knows how to ease
    the loss.
His Cross was heavy. He carried it to pay for all our sins.
We know not the reason, but He is there with all our friends."

Your faith will give you the ability to carry it high in the sky
And will make you trust Him, for only He
    knows the reason why.
You may feel like Job with all the troubles he had to bear.
You too will end up stronger in faith, for He was there to care.

Lift high your Cross and display it with pride,
For someday, what He did on His cross will take you
    on your heavenly ride.

Plant a Seed

Plant a seed and watch it grow.
How it will spread, only God will know.

Christ planted the seed so long ago.
And from it Christianity continues to grow.
From every smile and every word,
His message of love continues to be heard.

You will never know the place or time
Your actions will help someone His love to find.
So plant a seed of faith every chance you get.
It may be a friend or someone you just met.

The seeds you sow were given to you by your God.
They will grow in the field or they may grow in the sod.
Words are God's seeds He uses to let us know He is there.
So spread His seeds to those you love with joy and care.

Some seeds you sow may take longer to spread about,
But sooner or later His love will win out.
Our Lord taught us to sow our seeds with care,
For there are weeds to try to stop them everywhere.

Her Faith

Why do we mourn, for she has reached her goal?

From the very start, she saw her life unfold.

By taking the Master's hand, He led her all the way.

Though life was troubled, her faith in Him never would stray.

When blessings did shine the brightest, His praises she did give.

To be in His kingdom was the way her life was lived.

You could see it in her face and hear it in her voice.

What she thought He wanted was always her choice.

In trials and troubles, her faith always stood the test.

Now with Her Master, she has found the perfect rest.

Faith

Take Pride in God

Don't let your pride keep you off your knees when you pray.
Christ did not let His pride take Him off the cross
    that awful day.
Don't let your pride keep you from sharing your faith
    with others.
Christ said we should share our faith with all our
    sisters and brothers.

Don't ever let what others say weaken your faith in His love
Because He came to atone for all our sins and returned to
    His home above.

The pride you have in your faith should be shown
    in your smiling face.
Win or lose, we have already taken part in this earthly race.
We live in a world where sin is a permanent way to live,
But our faith in God lets us live with it, and if we stray,
    He will forgive.

The Light of God

What has happened to cause those smiles to make our faces
    so bright?
It is God's love that He gave us when He sent the spirit bringing
    His holy light.

If the light of Christ has shown in your heart today,
Let it reflect off your face to enlighten the souls of those
    you meet each day.

Our lives should not be spent in search of what's in it
    to satisfy me.
But should be spent telling others that seeking forgiveness
    will set them free.

From the cradle to the grave, God's arms are there to protect
    us all.
All we must do is accept this and acknowledge that Christ
    died for us all.

In a world so full of sin, we must always be alert and never
    let it touch our soul.
That was his message to Adam and Eve and what he tells
    us about being wary, both young and old.

Let God's light shine through your actions so others see
    what His love can do.
If they follow, they too will enjoy eternal love
    like me and you.

Faith

The Master's Eyes

I looked into the Master's eyes. And what did I see?
I saw a love that can never be attained by you or me.
His life was built on love, a love that will set us free.
He spread that love to everyone on the land and on the sea.

God sent Christ to the earth to bring His people out of the cold.
When He left us, He left it up to every living soul.
The love that was in His eyes can be felt each time we pray,
So we should look for this love each and every day.

Look into His eyes and see what you will find there.
You will find the answer to your every worldly care.
Look into His eyes and have faith He will call you someday.
Faith in His love will carry you safely home all the way.

The reflection in His eyes will always show us the way.
Just ask Him for His guidance each day when you stop to pray.

You Are Blessed

When have you stopped to thank God for the many blessings
    He showers on you?
He gave you to your parents whose love will be there
    to see you through.
He gave you the air to breathe and the food you enjoy too.
He sent His son to atone for any sins you commit,
    known or unknown.
He sent the Holy Spirit to stand beside you so you
    will never be alone.
He furnishes you the sunshine that gives you light and heat.
He gives you an assortment of fun things to do like toys
    or a drum to beat.
He leads you to your friends and others whom you can
    share your burdens and days with.
He's with you and taking care of you no matter how long
    He wants you to live.
God is with you. Just look around and see the beauty
    He created for all.
His love is for everyone now and forever, whether big or small.

Your Faith

Hold on to your faith, and to it always be true.

Whatever comes up, it is your faith that will get you through.

Your faith is the result of God's love for you.

Hold to it tightly so that doubt or hate will not make you blue.

Evil and greed might try to take faith's peace from your soul.

But your true faith will keep God's love in control.

Satan can take your health, your wealth, even your life.

True faith will bring you to heaven where there is no strife.

Your faith will always bring you God's peace and joy.

It must be kept close and near. Don't play with it like a toy.

Family and Special People

Fathers Are Loved

Here's to our Heavenly Father, the Maker of all.
He is there to help us get up whenever we fall.
He smiles with joy when we follow in His steps.
It is His peace that comes when nothing else helps.

What a wonderful model our earthly fathers have to follow.
He's a leader, a teacher, a guide, and a model of a good fellow.
God our Heavenly Father sets the standard to live by.
Let's honor our earthly fathers with love. It's the best buy.

We must love our fathers here and in heaven above.
So shower them all with a special gift of love.
Fathers are special. And I will tell you the reason why:
They help make us with the help from the Father in the Sky.

So today let's honor all fathers here and above,
With plenty of love like God sent on the wings of a dove.

Mother's Love

The love of a mother is like the love of God.
It will go with you the world over wherever you trod.

No matter the worry or pain you may cause,
It is always forgiven without ever a pause.
Mothers were given to you by God above
To show you the true meaning of the word *love*.

Whether young or old, you are always in her heart.
No matter what you do to her, you will always be a part.
Should she be near or gone far away,
Let her know now she's in your heart today.

Always remember you were God's gift for her to share.
Tell her how much of that love you will always bear.

Love Is a Sister

Sisters had to have come from God above
Because they are so full of His true love.

When the whole world seems to turn its back,
Your sister's love you will never lack.
The clouds may be dark and the rain may be bad.
But your sister's love is there to pick you up and make
    you glad.

Sisters come in all sizes and shapes like mothers,
But their main love is always for others.
So each day when you pray to God above,
Be sure to thank Him for the sisters you love.

Family and Special People

For Your Anniversary

Happy anniversary to you, whose love has proven so true.
This type of love is sought by many but found by so few.

They say marriages are made in heaven and arranged from above.
It is God who brought you together and gave you true love.

True love is rare and is found by a very few.
So cling to each other and share a love true.

Years may come, and many years will pass.
But your type of love is one that will last.

Golden Anniversary

Fifty years ago this very day,
This joyous couple set on their happy way.

There have been many highs and lows they have
    had to face.
But their trust was and is now in His grace.

The lives they have touched are spread far and wide,
But they know that in time of trouble, many will be
    at their side.

God brings people together in His own loving way.
And if we only listen to Him, this is the way it will stay.

Life is not a one-way street. This they know so true.
But with their faith in God, He has seen them through.

The love that lit their faces so many years ago
Can still be seen in their eyes. You can tell it is so.

Birthday Wish

This is the day God chose to send you to earth.

You brought much joy and happiness at your birth.

Let us hope that with each coming year,

Your life will be full of happiness and good cheer.

A happy birthday is wished for you this day.

May everything you wish for come your way.

Happy Birthday, Ellen

Here's to Ellen, a queen and a clown.
She has never turned her back on her hometown.

Her joy is to bring pleasure to others.
To her, all people are her sisters and brothers.

To make sure it's right, she did a show in bed.
Her only aim is that the right thing will be said.

She dances and does things and acts like a fool.
But when things get rough, she always remains cool.
We have watched her for years doing any kind of skit.
Now "The Ellen Show" seems to be her biggest hit.

Happy birthday, Ellen. May you have many more years.
We will still be watching with smiles or tears.
Here's to you with your soul of gold and your heart as big.
We will watch you till you're so old you'll have to wear a wig.

Happy Birthday, Shirley

Here's to Shirley, the love of our heart.
No matter where we go, it will never part.

Once you have met her, that love you will feel.
And in every encounter, you'll know it is real.
She always cares for others and not for herself.
Her love is true, not something off a shelf.

When times are bad, she is the first to be there
To give of her love. And she will always care.
May this birthday be the best she has known.
And may she receive more love than she ever has been shown.

Your Day

Joy, joy, you have a birthday!

What a blessing you were born on a special day.

God had a job He sent you to do.

And to that goal, you have always been true.

This is your day and will be forever.

Just hang on to His love in your every endeavor.

When things need to be done, we can count on you.

You always have a plan to see you through.

Over 80 in God's Care

God has blessed us with 80 or more years on this
    good earth.
We've seen many changes since our mothers gave us birth.

There have been wars, riots, and all kinds of disasters.
But nothing with God's love and grace we were not
    able to master.
There have been times of grief and sorrow.
But with His love, we always knew there would be
    a better tomorrow.

Through every day God has always been there at our side.
If we would always just pray, He would be there to guide.
Let's always hope we will have many more years to share.
And then gather in His heavenly home with those
    who are there.

Giving Thanks

Say Thank You

When have you just looked up to the sky and said,
    "Thank you for whom I am"?
For God has made us and put us where we are, even down
    to the smallest lamb.
He made us to fit His own plan and provided for
    our every need.
His only requirement is to trust Him. And every comment
    we must heed.

Each morning we should thank Him for a new day
And ask His guidance all the way.
His love is proven by the sun and the stars
And earns the words that we pray.

In His wisdom He knew we would be led by sin
    off His set path,
But He sent His son to atone for our sins. And His son
    gave His life on our behalf.
Each minute we have we should spend showing our thanks
    for His eternal love.
Telling everyone we meet about His peace and love, sent
    to us from heaven above.

Giving Thanks

Thanks for Today

It was God who put you in your mother's womb.
He will protect you through life to the tomb.

Take what He has given you and enjoy it every day.
Just take a moment to thank Him for this special day.

He gave His son to lead us into a useful life.
He even led us to find our husband or wife.

Trust His wisdom and love to lead you each day.
But always stop and thank Him for every blessing along the way.
The water we drink, the air we breathe are all gifts from God.
It's all His loving gifts, regardless of which path we have trod.

Today Is Today

There are no tomorrows and no yesterdays
Because everything that happens is happening today.

No one has ever seen a tomorrow, for its day is today.
Don't put off what you have to do. Do it right away.

There is no yesterday, for it has become today.
The more we try to wait, it seems to happen anyway.

Say what you want to say and say it today.
God in His wisdom never showed us tomorrow.
    It's always today.

What happened yesterday will never change, for it is today.
Don't delay until tomorrow. It will get done anyway.

God will send His love to us each and every day.
When you awake in the morning, thank God for another day.
When you close your eyes at night, thank Him when you pray.

Heaven and Angels

Heaven's Stairway

We are climbing the stairs to heaven. We must climb them every day.
We must keep climbing them if we want to reach our heavenly home someday.
We must climb those heavenly steps, for there is no shorter way.

Day by day and step by step. Upward we must always tread.
On we must go. Never looking back. Just living as our Master has said.

The stairway to heaven is crowded, and to temptations many a soul is lost.
We may stumble and trip. But we must go, for Christ has paid the cost.

Climbing that ragged stairway wasn't easy, even for our Master.
But with our faith in His word, He will enable us to make the climb a little faster.

Oh what joy when we march up those last few steps and enter our heavenly rest.
The climb will be short for some, longer for others. But things there will only be the best.

Climbing the steps to heaven is made easier when we pray.
For this means we are walking with Jesus every step of the way.

Angels Everywhere

Angels are God's helpers here on earth.
They start their work at all ages. Some even at birth.

You never know when you will meet them in their labors.
In a shop. Or it could be your local neighbors.

They come in all shapes and sizes,
But what they do will bring many surprises.

You meet them in all walks of your life.
Don't be surprised: it could be your husband or wife.

They don't go around with halos over their heads.
They just go and do whatever God has said.
Some were sent to sing when Christ was born.
It's said that life will end when Gabriel blows his horn.
We are never given a clue as to when that might be,
But angels' love has no strings because it is free.

God could be calling you to do His work today.
So grab your halo, and tell Him to show you the way.

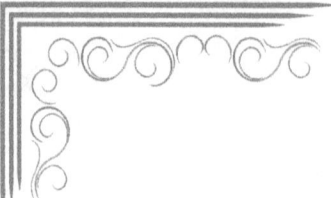

Keys

I found the keys to heaven, though they were not lost.
They were hanging next to Jesus when He was paying the cost.
The key to salvation and the key to the perfect reason for life
Can be found when you choose Jesus's way out of strife.

He hung on that cross because He knew it was the only way
To save all sinners who would come to believe someday.

We have been told the gates to heaven are sealed very tight.
The key that opens them has been hanging there in clear sight.
God sent His son to save a world that was wasting away in sin.
He said if they repented and truly had faith, He would let them in.

With faith and trust, we stare at that empty cross.
He died and has risen so that human life is not a complete loss.

Our Guardian Angel

He came into my life as a guardian, but he turned out to be
    a guardian angel.
We were meeting to discuss "the flight of honor" from
    every angle.
Even though we had never met, I felt his friendship
    from the start.
From his first words and actions, you could tell he took
    his guardianship to heart.

The flight was wonderful, well planned. Someone was there
    to fill our every care.
The crowd to welcome us home was the greatest thing.
Signs showing "Thank you for your service" were everywhere.
Billy was our guardian. And now he's our friend.
The comradeship we formed on April 17, 2010, will never end.

Our Home

Have you ever lain on the ground and watched the
    clouds float by
And wondered about your heavenly home in the sky?
Have you ever lain in a dark bed at night
And wondered if heaven would be a beautiful sight?

Our Lord told His followers of the things that were to be.
He said if we believed in Him, it would all be free.
God's love for His people should be known without a doubt,
For Christ told everyone what it was all about.

Love one another as He has loved thee.
His love for us will make us happy and free.
Love is the answer to every problem we face.
It will lead us home to our heavenly place.

Go tell it to those we meet on our way,
So they too can join us on that blessed day.

Love

Go Love Each Other

If you love me as I have loved you,
This will mean you will always be true.

When Jesus came, His one goal in life
Was for us to love each other without any strife.
"Love one another" is a very simple way to say,
"I love you as a brother and live it each day."
If everyone would do this,
What a wonderful way to live.
Life would be the very love that we give.

God sent His son to teach us the way.
Simply love one another each blessed day.
The disciples taught that we should love our neighbor.
This will bring peace and joy, which we all savor.

We should love everyone we meet. Not pick and choose.
If your love brings some to Jesus, what can we lose?
Love lifts all to a love from God above.
Give and receive a life filled with endless love.

Love

His Love Is Forever

Whether changing water to wine or eternal life,
His goal in life was to end everyone's strife.
He never looked for gain but only wanted to help others.
His message to all was to love each other since we are all
    sisters and brothers.

God sent Him to earth to tell all about His heavenly love
And how to live here to attain a place in our home above.
Love is the answer to solving our problems here on earth
And was proven to us all by Christ's wonderful birth.

God's love is shown to us every day that we live.
We can prove it every day. Not by what we receive
    but by what we give.
God's love is to be shared with those we meet every day.
It will last forever and it will never decay.

I Pray for You

When I wake up in the morning, I say a prayer for you.
I ask God to be with you in everything you do.
With this prayer I know He will guide you wherever you go.
I ask no other blessing, for He knows I love you so.

With my prayer I know you will feel Him there
And will take just a moment to tell Him how much you care.

I pray you will always care for others as He cares for you.

When my prayers are over, I have nothing else to fear,
For my heart is filled with a perfect peace so dear.
I stop and listen for His reply that will come very soon.
He grants my prayers as surely as a mother feeds her
    child with a spoon.

Love Is Forever

Where has the love gone that was shown at the
    manger birth?
Where has the love gone that angels sang,
    welcoming Him to this earth?
Where has the love gone shown by those
    He cured of their ills?
Where has the love gone that was shown by those
    He met walking up that awesome hill?
Where has the love gone that was shown when
    He hung on that cross?
Where has the love gone that was shown when the empty
    tomb proved there was no loss?
That love is here, but we are not looking for it where
    He sent us.
That love is here, but we are not giving Him our every trust.
God's love is and will always be without a bit of change.
God's love still reaches for us in the cities or on the
    wide open ranges.
Open your heart. Let Him enter in.
And He will forgive your every sin.

Love Is the Answer

Love is the answer to the problems we face.
It won't make you a winner, but it will keep you in the race.
Love can turn hate into caring for others.
It can teach us that we are all sisters or brothers.

Love can take sadness and turn it into joy.
It can make us like a child with a new toy.
Love makes us listen to those who are calling.
Love will lead you to help those who are falling.

Love can heal a heart that has been broken.
It is the truest words that were ever spoken.
Love can change the life even of a nonbeliever.
Love can soften the heart of the worst deceiver.

It was God's love for all the human race
That caused Him to send His son to set the pace.

Love can stop wars and end all need.
Love can stop lust and end greed.
Love is God's answer to all our prayers.
Love is God's way of saying that He cares.

No Ifs

If the world were filled with love,
    there would be no fear of tomorrow.
If the world were filled with love,
    there would be no sorrow.
If the world were filled with love,
    there would be no one living in hunger.
If the world were filled with love,
    there would be no room for anger.
If the world were filled with love,
    every face would wear a smile.
If the world were filled with love,
    we would never have to wait awhile.
If the world were filled with love,
    greed would hide its ugly face.
If the world were filled with love,
    everyone would not care about race.
If the world were filled with love,
    we would all live in God's grace.
If the world were filled with love,
    evil would leave without a trace.

God's love is the cure for all of mankind,
So let us pray that it will soon take over every mind.

Not for Sale

God's love is not for sale. It is free for you and me.
Christ paid the cost by dying on the cross for all to see.
Nothing we can do will ever atone for the deed He did.

All we have to do is trust and live as He has said.
His love is real and we must follow as He has led.

Go tell the world what He has done to set you free.
By your actions and words, everyone will be able to see.

In our lifetime we have choices that we all must make,
So pray for guidance in the choice of each course
    you will take.

God chose you for His kingdom and will always show
    you the way.
But you must look and listen for His direction each
    and every day.

Sometimes life is dark, but His love is always
    shining ahead.
Have faith and trust, and to your heavenly home
    you will be led.

Love

Open Your Treasures

You have many treasures, mostly still locked in your brain.
Dig in. Open up. Let your love of God fall like rain.
Go out today and let others know what God has given you.
Tell others of your treasures He gave you that no one
    ever knew.

What is the love of God if you don't spread it around?
Spread it everywhere you go. In the big city
    or the small town.

What if God had not sent His son to set us free from sin?
Tell all you meet what Christ has done for you and
    ask them to join in.
In a world filled with sin, it's time to share His love to all.
Open your hidden treasures today and answer
    the Master's call.

Out With Hate

Hate must go or God's love cannot be found.
For when hate moves in, love will move out of town.
Hate will consume you both body and soul.
At the mention of the word, you can see evil unfold.

Hate is one thing you will not find in your heavenly
    home above
Because it is kept out by God's grace and outgoing love.
Hate causes problems in families and in every nation
And cannot be overcome except by God's love
    and salvation.

Hate started with Cain and Abel and seems to grow
    every day.
But we can stop this growth by watching what we say.
It can be stopped. The remedy is as simple as it can be.
Just spread God's love to everyone you may see.

Special Grace

We can never earn God's grace and love.
It comes freely to all from heaven above.
He created mankind for His own joy,
And His love is renewed in each newborn girl or boy.

God's love has no strings to bind you to Him.
He only asks you to love Him with all your vigor and vim.
With each day He gives you the chance to tell of His grace.
So tell of His love and care to all you may face.

His love will guide you from morning to night.
Just keep His commandments as your only light.
Each day you live is a special gift just for you.
Use each day for His glory in all that you may do.

Take His hand and let Him lead you on life's busy trail.
Do this and whatever you face, with Him you can never fail.
God's love is here, so trust Him each day.
Jesus showed this and told you not to stray.

Stop—Look—Listen

We should all stop for a moment and talk of God's love.
We should listen as He tells of our home above.

We should look at all the things God has done for
    each of us.
We should thank Him for giving us our faith and trust.

We should always be telling others about how we
    are cared for.
How listening to His messages should be a blessing,
    not a bore.
How He leads us to share our blessings to those in need.
How to tell everyone that having faith in Him
    is planting a seed.

Stop, look, and listen as you travel along life's busy highway.
You may never really know what happens when
    you have your say.
God uses us all so often, we have been told.
The rich, the poor, the meek, and the bold.

Love

Wedding Hope

As they stand at the altar this very day,
Let us hope they know what God has had to say.
They were born in different areas and raised in different ways.
But God has brought them together to share their days.

They had spent their lives miles apart,
But it was God who led them from the start.

As they are joined together by word and deed,
Let them never forget who planted the seed.
Husbands and wives are given to each other by God
And should always love each other, as they are loved by God.

What the future will hold, no one will know.
But the love they have for each other is all that will show.

What Love?

You wake up in the morning. But you do not know when
God will call your name and say, "This is the end."

You will never know how many lives you may touch.
You will never know that your words and actions
    did so much.
Day in and day out, your thoughts went out to others.
Everyone was treated like sisters or brothers.

God gives us the way we should always love.
He sent it to us when He sent us His son from above.
God's love was given with no strings attached.
Our ability to give love like Him will never
    be matched.

Love

Yours

We are Yours. What else is there to say?
You show Your love each and every day.
We awake in the morning to the gift of another day.
We go to bed at night knowing You have taken our sins away.
Oh, what joy we receive from Your untiring love.
It makes us ready for seeing You in Your home above.

God has made us as different as night and day.
But we all have to accept the trials we face along the way.
Lord, You sent Your son to guide us along the trail.
You know that following His ways, we cannot fail.
You chose us to be Your witnesses to those we meet
    along the way.
You reward us with Your love each time we stop to pray.

You are my God and the Maker of us all.
Let us sing Your praises on this celestial ball.
Make us ready for Your kingdom when it comes to be.
You have made everything from the heavens to the sea.

Don't Lose It

The child has been born. God's love again has been shown.

What will it mean? Will a new era begin to dawn?

This gift of God's love was given to save all mankind.

But we must accept this gift and let it fill our minds.

God gave us this gift, but He will not force us to take it.

We must live it and let it rule every act of our Spirit.

God fulfilled the scriptures that were written so long ago.

Now we must tell everyone we meet His love for us will flow.

Don't throw this gift away as so many have done.

Keep it in your heart, and share it with meaning to everyone.

Prayer

God Is Here

Who listens to your every prayer from anywhere
And with His answer says, "Yes, I care"?
Who sent His son to show He loves us all
And is there to help you when your faith begins to stall?
Who brings the freshness of every morn
And gives you strength when in sadness you mourn?

God is there at early dawn to brighten your day.
He is there watching over you in His loving way.
God is with you from the cradle to the grave.
And with His love He assures you that you are His to save.

So awake each day with a prayer of thanks for what
    He has done.
Then close each night with a prayer that His battle
    with evil will soon be done.

Pray and Listen

When we pray we usually talk to God or just listen
    to what He has to say.
We tell Him all our troubles, then go on with other things
    we are doing that day.

Pray when it is quiet and nothing else is there to take
    your mind away.
Tell Him everything, for He already knows all
    your problems anyway.

When you are talking to God, it is not to some machine,
    so listen for His reply.
Listen to what you hear Him say. Then act on
    what He says. It's always true. Never a lie.

God will act. And sometimes we do not like what
    He will do or say.
Prayer is always a two-way talk. We both should expect
    action in His holy way.

Every prayer should start with thanks for what
    He has done,
Then end with us listening to Him telling us just how
    His will must be done.

Professions

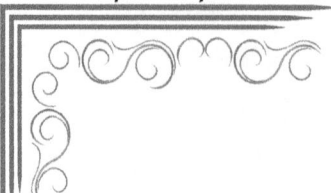

A Man of Music

Oh what a blessing that came our way
When he joined our church and said, "I want to play."
His love for music is what it's all about.
His love of teaching it to others is never in doubt.

The instruments he uses are always his choice.
He masters them all, to match any voice.
The choirs he leads with a skill so great,
You often wonder what sounds he'll create.

He reaches in his music and pulls out a sheet.
The next job is to teach his choirs the right beat.
His music leads our service week after week.
The specials he chooses always lead us to a peak.

His knowledge of church music is a known fact.
And his love for teaching others, you can see in every act.
God has blessed him with a talent that passes the test.
We know wherever he goes, they will enjoy the best.

Professions

The Grasshoppers Are A-Comin'

Out of the bush leagues they came jumping to play.
They hopped onto the field with a shout to get the game
    under way.
The New Horizon Field was just what it was supposed to be.
A wonderful new place for their fans to come and see.

With dreams that come in the spring each year.
With their bats and gloves, they play as the fans start
    to cheer.
Oh what a joy they hope the season will bring.
They play their hearts out and listen to hear the praises
    their fans will sing.

They jump and hop and run all over the field so green
Their only goal is to give the fans the best game they've
    ever seen.
When the season is over and the dust has settled down,
They hope that on the flagpole, the championship flag
    will be found.

Main Ingredients

Cooks and bakers come in all sizes, both young and old.
But they are always amazed at how their works will unfold.

With every recipe they use, every step must be followed to
    the very end.
Every ingredient added. And everything must be in the
    final blend.

You cook and bake to share with those you care about.
By following each recipe, you know without a doubt it
    will turn out.

Some recipes are passed from age to age without a single
    item of change.
Remember, it's your creation that is going to come out
    of the range.

The main ingredients in all we cook or bake should be love
    and care
And a prayer of thanks to God who made all we needed
    and made sure it was there.

Mission Developer

He came to town fresh out of the seminary.
He was going to save every soul except those in the cemetery.
He gathered his flock wherever he could find them.
He knocked on doors. And when they would talk he said,
    "Amen."

The flock that he gathered will go on forever,
Because he left the Holy Spirit behind in his endeavor.
The word he spread was like the flame of old.
He faced each problem with a spirit so bold.

They would meet wherever a room could be found.
For it was God's word that he wanted to spread around.
He would lead his flock until he felt his work was done.
Then he would leave them to build another one.

The lives he touched throughout those years of toil
Would be like counting the grains in a ton of soil.
The flocks he gathered keep going their way.
For they know it is God's will that they obey.

His service was long and his time well spent.
But now he's enjoying the retirement that God has sent.

Our Doctor

Why do we mourn, for he has reached his goal?
From the start he could see his life unfold.
By taking his Master's hand, He led him all the way.
Though life was troubled, his faith and trust
    never would stray.

When the people came to him with their aches
    and their pains,
With his knowledge of medicine he made them feel
    like new again.
He studied hard day and night to make sure his decisions
    were the best.
His only goal was to see that his patients were always well
    enough to pass his test.

You could see it in his face and hear it in his voice.
What he thought God wanted was always his choice.
In trials and troubles, his faith would always stand the test.
Now with his Master, he has found the perfect rest.

Questioning

Are You Still Seeking?

God sent you a Savior when He sent His only son.
Just place your trust in Him and your trip has begun.
When you are the lowest, He will be your way out.
Believe in His words. Never leave room for a doubt.

Following His way will not always be so easy to do.
Don't let a little doubt stop you, for He's always with you.
In the air or in a cave deep under the ground,
Through your faith and trust His love will be found.

God threw out the lifeline so everyone is brought to Him.
It comes to you in the Bible and sometimes in a hymn.
Always reach out to others, and they too will be in His hands.
His love for us is greater than all the grains of sand.

The kingdom of God can't be earned but comes only
    by His grace.
Believe, trust, and live in His faith. And you will meet
    Him face-to-face.

Have You Ever Thought…?

Have you ever thought what an artist our God really is?
He made every tree. And the pattern is really His.
He painted every flower and gave it its special shape.
He created all the animals from the zebra to the ape.

He set the mountains in their ranges where they should be.
He placed the oceans in their depths and set the waters free.
He made people like you and me and sent us on our way.
He said when you have a problem you cannot solve,
    just stop and pray.

The trees are still growing and the mountains still
    stand in place.
But the people seem to be trying to end the human race.
Prayer is the only answer to it all,
So stop and listen for the Master's call.

Hearing God

Have you heard Him today as you travel along your way?
Would you know Him or listen to what He had to say?
His messages come to us in many different ways.
We may be listening to others or we may be giving
    Him praise.

God talked to man even before He sent His son.
Stop and listen to what He has to say. You could be the one.
You hear His message when you listen to a sermon
    on Sunday morn.
You can even hear Him when someone blows a horn.

He not only speaks to us in the many words we hear.
You can even hear Him in the eyes of those you hold dear.
He taught us He would be with us wherever we go.
Open up to His love and you see that it is so.

His Reason

Have you ever stopped to think how life would be
Had the Good Guy not come and died upon a tree?
He was sent by His father to atone for our sins.
It was a job that He wouldn't be asked to do again.
He walked the countryside urging people to repent.
That was His message. The reason He was sent.

This is the reason for our troubled world today:
We lack the faith to live by the words He had to say.
The problem is we must meet these troubles face-to-face,
Remembering that all things can be solved by believing
    in His grace.
God has the answer to our every prayer.
We must take prayers to Him and leave them there.

If God Should Go On Strike

How good it is that God above has never gone on strike
Because He was not treated fairly in things He didn't like.

If only once He'd given up and said, "That's it. I'm through!
I've had enough of those on earth, so this is what I'll do.
I'll give my orders to the sun to cut off the heat supply.
And to the moon to give no more light.
    And run the oceans dry.
Then just to make things really tough and put the
    pressure on,
Turn off the vital oxygen till every breath is gone!"

You know He would be justified, if fairness were the game.
For no one has been more abused or met with more disdain
Than God. And yet He carried on, supplying you and me
With all the favors of His grace. And everything for free.

Men say they want a better deal, and so on strike they go.
But what a deal we've given God to whom all things we owe.
We don't care whom we hurt to gain the things we like.
But what a mess we'd all be in, if God should go on strike.

If He Came Today

If He came to earth today,
What would He have to say?
Like the apostles of old, He would say,
"Repent and go on your way."
Like His reason for coming to earth years ago.
"Repent. Trust me since I have told you the way to go."

His message remains the same today, tomorrow,
    throughout all the years.
"Love each other and show everyone there are those who care."
His life was a message of love no one has ever known.
His love can help you make dust out of the hardest stone.

Time has passed and years have gone by, but His love
    remains the same.
Faith, hope, and love are the only ways to play life's game.
Evil exists and is always trying to rule your life.
But faith and love will help you overcome all the evil vices.

Christ is here and lives in us each and every day.
He will never forsake us, no matter how we may stray.
His mission will never change and will always be the only way.
Love and trust Him in all you do and say each and every day.

The Answer

How many times are you asked, "What's wrong
    with the world today?"
The answer is simple: we just don't take time to
    stop and pray.
Prayer can bring the answer if we will just listen to
    what He has to say.
But we usually pray, then try to solve things in our own way.

The evil that seems to be trying to rule all our lives today
Can be ended by God's love if we let Him—through faith—
    have His way.
Many lives are lost to the evil that seems to have no end.
The answer is to spread His love to those we meet.
    Foe or friend.

God's love is the answer to each prayer we can ever say.
It will mean more to us every time we try to give it away.

What Is Life About?

What is this life we live each day all about?
It must be lived filled with love and never a doubt.
Life is God's creation, no matter what some may say.
And if we listen to His words, He will guide us every day.
In His wisdom He made everything to show His love
    in its own way.

When mankind turned from His love and began to sin,
He sent His son to bring us back to His love once again.

We should live this life reflecting His love on our faces.
Nothing we have done will earn our salvation. It's only
    by His grace.
Each day should be spent telling others what God
    has done for you.
Let your every action show your faith in His word is true.

Where Is God?

When the sun rises in the morning, God is there.
If you stub your toe and want to cry, He says, "I care."

When sorrow brings you to sob, His love
    will see you to its end.
Should all your friends not be there, He will say,
    "I am also your friend."

When you want to hear someone say, "I love you so much,"
Just stand there and wait for His loving touch.

When you feel all alone and no one else seems to care,
He will be close and say, "I am here, your problems to share."

Never fear. Just hold onto your faith to be true.
By His love and grace, He will always see you through.

Who Is He?

Jesus asks you this question every day.
He wants to know what you have to say.
"What do you think I'm trying to say to you?
Can I count on you to see Me through?
Will you be there when times are trying?
Would you have been there when I was dying?"

He wants to know, "How strong is your love?
Will you really claim your home in heaven above?"

He put His disciples to this very test.
And each day we must answer more or less.

The way we love each other every day
Gives Him our answer in a very active way.
Is He your Lord and Savior as Peter has said?
Or will you be waiting to see what is ahead?

He just wants to know where you will make your stand.
He wants to know if you will join His joyous band.
The choice is yours to make. No one else can do it.
Make the choice and in heaven with Him you will sit.

Reflections

Blessed Peace

We feel His peace pass over us whenever we fall on our knees.
We know it will stay if only His will we try to please.
This blessed peace can only be found
When we realize God's presence is all around.
He brings it to us so rest can be assured.
His peace can see to it that our problems are endured.

Yes, we can find that peace in no other way.
But by taking our problems to Him as we pray,
His peace can be found both night and day.
It will go with you every step of the way.

His peace can't be bought because it is free.
It was paid for that day when He hung on that tree.
This peace comes with the blessed assurance
If it is His word that is our only influence.
He granted it to His disciples so long ago.
And it is ours if we take Him with us wherever we go.

God Is Everywhere

You can see Him in the eagles that soar in the sky.
You can see Him in the apples baked in a pie.
You can see Him in the snowflakes as they fall.
You can see Him in the faces you see at the mall.

You can see Him in the flowers that bloom in the spring.
You can see Him in the birds as they sing.
You can see Him in the fish that swim in the sea.
You can see Him in a creature as small as a bee.

You can see Him in a baby at its birth.
You can see Him in everything on earth.
You can see Him in the trees as they grow so tall.
You can see Him in the colors of the leaves as they fall.

You can see Him in the morning's early light.
You can see Him at sunset, at the beginning of the night.

Have a Little Talk With God Each Day

Have a little talk with God each day.
Stop and listen to what He has to say.
I have tried to do this since my mother taught me to pray.
Each morning I thank Him and listen to hear what
    He might say.

His line is never busy, no matter when or where you call.
He is always ready to answer. Spring, summer, winter, fall.
Be sure what you ask for, you really want to know.
He will always answer, not always the way you want
    it to be so.

His answer will be honest and sometimes put you to a test.
If you will only trust Him, His way is always the best.

In life, you will face many problems you cannot solve.
But share them with the Lord, and they will soon dissolve.
He knows your every problem. He knows your every care.
So talk to Him about them and soon they will be His to bear.

How needless it is to worry. How needless it is to doubt.
Just take them to God, for He knows what they are all about.

His Hands

If His hands are upon you, nothing else can bother,
For you will be protected by your loving heavenly Father.
The world is in His ever-loving hands.
And only He knows His eternal plans.

Sin and evil will be wherever we go.
Peace and love are what He will always show.
His hands will clear away the hurt and pain,
And lead you down that heavenly lane.

No sin, no sorrow will be in your home above.
Only happiness that will be given by His love.
Like Jesus who obeyed His every word,
Our faith will let us be as free as a bird.

Remembering September 11, 2001

September 11, 2001, started like every other day that
    God does send.
But no one could have dreamed just how it would
    come to an end.
People left home and were busy at their jobs
    doing their things,
Unaware of the havoc that was approaching on evil wings.

One tower. Then two. The madmen flew the planes into
    both the towers so tall,
Killing thousands of people—young and old—and causing
    both towers to fall.
On the ground help poured in without fear, trying to
    get many out.
They did the jobs they were taught to do, going up stairs
    without a doubt.

Many lives were lost because a few people were filled
    with evil and hate.
But sooner or later each will receive their own due fate.
Here's a thank you to all who lost their lives reaching out to
    friend or stranger.
If you lost a loved one, be relieved now, for they
    aren't facing any danger.

Start Now

Don't put off until tomorrow.
It must be done today.
Go to Christ with all your problems
And He can take them away.

He paid for our sins with His death
On that awful cross.
If we believe this, His life was our win
And to Satan it was a loss.

Every day we should reach out and touch
Someone in Christ's name.
When you act in His name, whomever you touch
Will never be the same.

Your life is limited, so don't miss a chance
To tell what His love means to you.
And tell it in a way that whomever hears it
Will know it is true.

Always be looking for someone to share His
Message of love and hope.
For if they will trust in His words, with all of life's
Problems they will be able to cope.

Sweet Rest

How many times a day do you hear someone say,
    "I'm so tired I don't know what to do?"
God has given us the answer, but we will not listen and
    keep trying to get through.
He said, "Come with me, all you who are weary,
    and I will give you peace and rest."
We just keep on with our trials and worries,
    never thinking His words are the best.

God made man. God provided for his needs, water, food.
    And that he had plenty of rest.
Then evil came along and convinced man to put God's
    rules to a test.
Since then, man has had to struggle to survive and
    live by his labor.
Now we try to solve our problems—not by His word—but
    with our saber.

When we are tired, we should go to God for His love
    and rest.
Going to Him in our prayers and in faith, believing that
    He will help us do what's best.

Your Memories

Memories are what this life is all about.
They can help you overcome any sort of doubt
When they happen, it's over and will never be the same.
The event is finished, but the outcome is part of the game.

Some memories are sad and tattered with age.
Some are happy, and their joy will fill many a page.
Some are from when you were young and full of dreams.
Some fill your heart so tightly it almost bursts at the seams.

Remember the wonderful sights when you were a child.
Memories of your youth when you were a little wild.
Remember the excitement of those early Christmas charms.
Memories of the love found in your parent's arms.

Memories of snowflakes as they fell to the ground.
Remember walking with your true love all over town.
Memories of the young bride walking down the aisle.
Remembering the groom watching with a beaming smile.

The things you see, the things that you feel
Will in your memories be one great deal.
Years will come and years will go by fast.
But it is your memories that will make them last.

Salvation

A Spot in Your Heart

Save a spot in your heart for God to fit in.
There is no other way for Him to remove your sin.
Every day He wants to be with you,
So save Him a place with a love so true.

From the light of the morning to the dark of night,
He will be there to protect you with all His might.
He will not force His love upon you against your will,
But He's always around just over the next hill.

He gave His word that He would always be at your side.
And He will know that to no one has He ever lied.
Save that spot, for you never know when God will show.
In a flash of a light. Or day. Or night. We never know.

God waits in your heart so He can guide your soul.
Just let Him in and listen to what you are told.
Open your heart to those you meet every day,
But save a spot for God to be there to stay.

Salvation

Change Must Come

Everyone is asking, "How can we stop this evil that is
     happening everywhere?"
There can be a change, but everyone must do their share.
We all must turn and listen to what Christ has told us to do.
By following His words, that is the only way we know
     to be true.

No one is perfect. We all are tempted more each day.
But we never know whom we might change by what we say.

God gave us life, and it should be His to use.
We have His promise and love, but we never
     should use it to force or abuse.
We know His love and should be freely giving it to others.
For all we meet each day are our sisters and brothers.

Our faith in Christ can never be taken away.
Just share it with others and it will grow stronger every day.

His Will Must Be Done

When you accept Him as your Lord and Savior,
It must be with all your heart, soul, and labor.
There can't be a doubt or a thought as to why.
You must give Him your all. Never ever wonder; only try.

With your faith set in Him, look all problems in the face,
Believing in His promise and trusting in His grace.
He gave you your life and protects you in every way.
So live up to His love and share it with others every day.

By giving it to others, it will be stronger in every matter.
Whatever comes your way, His love will not let it shatter.
He said, "Come unto Me." And this is what you have done.
So go plant your seeds of faith so they will grow for everyone.

Live your faith and never let doubt enter your mind.
His love for you is big enough for you and all mankind.

If the Lord Came Today

We all need to stop and think, *If God came today,*
    where would we stand?
Could we say, "Yes, Lord, I am ready. I try to obey
    your every command"?
We also might wonder what our neighbor's answer
    would be.
But it is not for us to judge, for only God will decide.
    Not you or me.

He wants us all in His heavenly home, but it is left to us.
    His will to obey.
He sent His son to lead the way. But it is God who will have
    the final say.

We should always share our faith in His promise with all
    we meet along the way,
Because this could be the day He comes. We want
    everyone to join us on that day.
Let us pray for all from morning to night, that we can aid
    Him in His eternal fight.
For God shall win and we shall join Him here.
    There is never morning or night.

No Room

There is always room in God's home on high.
If we follow the right path, we will reach it by and by.

With the birth of a small child in a barn,
God assured us of a room in His home that will be warm.
Millions celebrate this birth with love and care.
But their hearts are empty because sins are there.
This child lived and died, these sins to take away.
Yet many fail to listen and look for another way.

Why can't we love each other as we do this special day?
We should reach out to everyone we meet along the way.
God sent His love and redemption to all.
All we have to do is believe and answer His call.
Reach out and help someone toward their heavenly home.
Let your heart be filled with love and kindness
    wherever you roam.

Salvation

Now Is the Time

We cannot wait till tomorrow. We must act today.
We are not promised tomorrow, so we must
     turn to God and pray.
He has promised to be with us always. All we have to do is trust,
Tell everyone about our faith, and always living it is a must.

Everything we do each day is how people will judge us
     in how we follow His way.
Just trust and live each day the way He would have us to play.
His ways are hard. And we often will stray, but for our sins
     He's already paid.
We live our life sharing our faith with others. We never
     let our faith fade.

Evil will be around us each day. How and where
     we just don't know.
Our protection is to trust and pray. And in our lives it will show.
We never should run from evil. But we should stand up and fight,
Because with faith we know that nothing can stand up
     to His might.

This is God's world. And he tells us so in the rising
     of the sun each day.
We have nothing to fear as long as we trust in what He has to say.

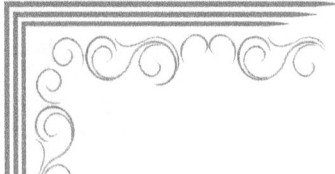

Our Salvation

Salvation cannot be bought, earned, or even won.
It was given to us as a gift by God's only son.
What made Him divine was not changing water into wine.
It was His willingness to die on the cross for all mankind.

His love was first shown in His coming to earth
And was proven to be true at His Easter rebirth.
The love He gave had never been known by anyone before.
That is why His followers love Him and His every act adore.

From the cradle to the tomb, His love was given
    for all to share.
He spread His word of love and goodwill to all
    who would care.
Unless Christ and His love are filling every heart,
Evil and sin will always take a part.

Rise and Shine

Rise and shine. The Lord is on the way.
This is and was the call of prophets of every day.
We are urged to live as if this were the last day.
Be prepared and urge others to do so in all you say.

Jesus taught us we do not know the day or the hour.
That he will return in all His glory and power.
Each of our days is numbered and we know not how many.
We may face problems, then again not so many.

Stop and smell the flowers as you live each day,
For He has given them to you. So thank Him as you pray.
Life is filled with blessings in so many ways,
So stop and count them. And give Him His praise.

So rise and shine to God's gift each morning
For all the surprises He has at the dawning.
Praise the Lord for the beauty He has made.
Forever keep your faith and never let it fade.

Simple Life

Roses are red. Violets are blue. Christ came
    to save me and you.
While the rhyme is simple, its meaning is so very true.

Jesus was sent by His father to save us from our sin.
He could have stayed in heaven. And His pain
    would not have had to begin.
Life is just as simple as the rhyme you just read.
Your faith will take you to be with Him just as He said.

God's love is as simple as the easiest nursery rhyme.
Reach out and He is with you through faith all the time.
God reached out and called you the day you were born.
Christ paid for your sins when He wore the crown
    made of a thorn.

God's love is yours. All you have to do is say yes.
By living a life of faithfulness, you have passed the test.

Seasons

A Christmas Prayer for You

That God will give you a peace only His son can bring.

That He will give you the knowledge to know
    it is the real thing.

That He will fill you with true love for all mankind.

That you will find a peace that many seek, but cannot find.

That He will give you the power to see the gift
    He has given you.

That to this gift your life will always be true.

Christmas

Seasons

A Message

It all began that happy day when the Christ Child was born.
And He lived a life of love until he died wearing His crown
    of thorns.

He was sent to bring God's people back to His ways.
He told His story of how God loved His people for days
    and days.
From God's promise to Abraham to lead him to a promised land.
It was always a hard message for some people to understand.

The message is simple: I made you and I will always love you.
He says this to everyone, not just a selected few.
Christ—like God—only wanted His people to remain
    loyal and true,
Believing that with true faith, His love is there to see
    you through.

Christmas

A Christmas Thought

'Tis the season of happiness and good cheer.
We shower our love on those we hold dear.
With lights strung from windows and walls
And shouts of greetings extended to all.
The gifts are all wrapped and the tags in place.
Now we wait to see the smiles to appear on each face.
The tree is trimmed with tinsel and lights so bright.
There's an angel perched on top so it is in everyone's sight.

In this season of giving, let us always keep in mind
The gift God has given to all of mankind.
It was a cold winter night in a manger so small
When God gave the gift that would benefit all.
The angels in heaven sang their hymns of joy.
The shepherds with their flocks searched for the boy.
In this season of joy when love seems to prevail,
Let us show this love in the greatest detail.

From a humble beginning, He became King and Lord,
Ending up giving His life for a troubled horde.
When the gifts are passed around, let us not forget
    the lowly few.
Let us always share the love He gave to me and you.

Christmas

Peace on earth can come, but it must have a start
That must come from the depths of each and every heart.
May this season fill us with love throughout the year,
Like the love that was shown at that birth we hold so dear.

Christmas

Believe in Him

This is Christmas, the time when Christ was born.
This is Christmas. This is when He was welcomed
    by every heavenly horn.
This is Christmas. This is the time God came to Earth.
This is Christmas, and we should pass God's love
    to everyone.
This is Christmas, a time to believe His every word
    was sent for you.
This is Christmas, a time to tell others of God's love so true.
This is Christmas, a time to tell all about the sacred story.
This is Christmas, a time to tell all of His rise to glory.
This is Christmas, a time for all believers to sing and shout.
Tell it everywhere what Christ's love is all about.

Christmas

Christ Must

What have they done to Christmas, the day of
    our Savior's birth?
The way some are acting, they want to imply it is
    all a myth.
The greatest gift ever given came to earth that blessed day.
A gift so precious that the angels had to stop and pray.
A gift of love with no strings attached.
A gift of love so pure it has never been matched.
The angels sang in the heavens above
And the shepherds came to see this child of love.

His life was short, but well spent.
His only call was for us to repent.
The time has come for all of us to say,
"You must put Christ back into this day.
It was Christ who came, God's words to extol.
His love was for all, both young and old."
Christ must be the center of this celebration.
Let us start now to tell it to every nation.

Getting Ready

As we near the holiday season, we need to stop and think.
Every gift from God has a very special link.

The early settlers stopped to thank God for his
    many blessings.
Surely, from their actions we should have learned
    many lessons.
We should stop and honor those who fought
    for our freedom,
And stop daily to thank Christ who prepared the way to
    His kingdom.

Every day we can do something to make someone
    a little better.
It could be a prayer, a call, a smile, or a friendly letter.
Soon our church service will be getting us ready for
    the Holy Season.
Let's all invite someone to come with us to learn the reason.

Christmas

God's Christmas Plan

The birth of Christ on that joyous day

Was offset by the sorrow felt when He was taken away.

Choirs of angels sang to announce His birth.

It was God's way to save his believers here on earth.

Like each of us, Jesus was born and He also died.

But thanks to God's mercy, we didn't have to hang by His side.

The joy of Christmas was all in God's plan for our eternal life.

A day that was His second birth on Easter settled all the strife.

God's Season

The angels sang to tell all of the Christ Child's birth.
The Magi traveled from afar to welcome Him to earth.
God sent His son to show how much we are in His love.
Christ's job was to guide us on the path to heaven above.

Christ gave us the gift in the form of eternal life.
We were His chosen as we choose our husband or wife.
The love that God showed to all so long ago
Is the same love He still wants us to feel and know.

Yes, we received that wonderful gift that special day.
Now we must give it to others in our special way.
Christ is the reason for this blessed season.
And we should love our fellowman for the same reason.

The giving of gifts at this season was to show their love,
And is the same as the love we receive on the wings
    of a dove.
We show our love by giving gifts to loved ones here
    on earth.
Let us not forget to shout thanks for that great birth.

God's love comes to us each and every day.
We should pass it on to those we meet along the way.

Christmas

He Was Born

Long ago and so far away, Christ was born in a manger.
His birth was foretold, so He did not come as a stranger.
His birthplace was lit by a star so bright.
It guided the Wise Men who were searching for this sight.
Over the years, there have been billions who gave birth.
But not one of them has brought so much to earth.

His life was short compared to the average today.
He has affected so many in every sort of way.
His life was humble. And he never traveled too far.
Though He never sought it, whatever He did He was
    always the star.
His life was and still is in service for others.
If you believe in Him, you become one of His brothers.

Though He suffered and died, He never did falter.
You will feel His presence when you join Him at the altar.
His birth is celebrated around the world each year.
Don't you often wonder what this world would be like
    if He had not been here?

Christmas

It All Starts Now

Now is the time when God decided to save the earth.
It is the season to celebrate our Savior's birth.
He was born in a manger so small and so bare,
Since there was no room in the inn that they could spare.

From birth to death His message was for us to love
    each other.
Prepare for our heavenly home where we will all be
    sisters and brothers.
The way we celebrate has changed, but the message
    is the same.
Love one another and we all will be welcomed to His home.

Let us all reach out and share His love so true.
May His peace fall on each heart. That includes me and you.

Christmas

Oh What a Gift

Oh what a gift our God gave that wonderful winter day.
A gift so wonderful the angels all sang and a new star
 appeared that day.
Unlike the gifts that others give, it never goes away.

The peace of mind that Christ has given will be forever.
All we need to do is accept His love and pass it on forever.
Gifts from man come and go, but none will ever compare
To a gift of love and hope that we can always share.

A gift so lasting over all the years. And it will never fail.
It's with you and available wherever your boat of life might sail.
Gifts are given for every reason, but nothing like this:
Christ came to earth for no other reason than our happiness
 and heavenly bliss.

Christmas

The Reason for the Season

As we approach the holiday season, we must remember
 the reason.
Christ came to earth for our salvation and no other reason.
He gave His life for all who believe and follow His way.
We should share our faith in Him to those we meet each day.

The love and joy we share with all at this time of year
Should show to all we meet that His birth was to fill us
 with cheer.
The hope He spread throughout His life should be
 shared by all.
Tell how the angels did sing and the Wise Men
 made their call.

This is a season for love and joy for a child born in a manger.
Reach out and share it to both a friend and a stranger.
Love is what life on this earth is all about.
Christ proved God's love beyond any doubt.

Christmas

The Season

You are the reason for this blessed season.
Yes, from God for you was the only reason.
His love for you was why He sent His son to earth.
It was in His love for you that He arranged the virgin birth.
It is personal, it is real, and it was just for you.
God gave you a way by showing His love so true.

The most wonderful gift was born in a manger.
It was God's way to keep you out of danger.
The angels sang announcing His birth.
The Wise Men came to welcome Him to earth.
A star shone brightly over the crib used for His bed,
Proving God's love for you just as He had said.

What better gift could God give to show His love for you?
He sent His son to secure eternal life for the faithful few.
Should someone ask you the reason for the special season,
Tell them it was God's love for them and no other reason.

Christmas

The Wise Still Seek

The child has been born. The Wise Men have come and gone.
Jesus has lived on earth and gone to His heavenly home.
He urged us to love each other, but this has not come about.
There are those who will try to fill your heart with
    hate and doubt.

Jesus lived here and died so we could be with Him in His
    home above.
God knew this was a sinful place, so He sent His son in love.
Our sins have been forgiven and He awaits us
    with open arms,
To spend eternity filled with His love free from all that harm.

Seek Him and follow His loving ways so we too can
    join Him someday.
Love and be loved each and every day. And show
    your love when you pray.

Christmas

A New Year

We know not the hour. We know not the day.
But Christ has told us to be prepared in every way.

Each New Year we set plans for another year.
We head into the future with our faith, not fear.
As you set your goals for the coming year,
Pray to God for love for those you hold so dear.

Love is the answer to whatever you might ask.
Love is what enables us to do the hardest task.
Love is what lets you face the future without a care.
God's love is waiting for you when you get there.

The New Year will bring joy, worry, and despair.
Faith and God's love will get you through with plenty to share.

New Year

Starting Right

Let's start the New Year filled with Christ's love and joy.
God has given us the key to our future in the form
    of a little boy.

Don't let the caring and love leave us as we go into
    the New Year.
Wherever the word of Christ is spread, it will stop
    a sorrowing tear.
Let us start each day as if starting a whole new life
By praying to God to end all the sinful hate and strife.
Oh, what a wonderful place the earth would be if
    we would just love each other.
God gave us His son to prove that love,
    so let's share it with sisters and brothers.

Let us start this year with a vow to serve our Lord
    in all we do.
Remember His son lived and died to ensure paradise
    for me and you.

New Year

A Lenten Prayer

Lord, let the cross on my brow

Remind me of the blood You shed.

Remind me of the unsaid prayer.

Remind me to pray for a friend.

Remind me to be thankful for each day.

Remind me to help someone each day.

Remind me to stop and listen for directions on my way.

Remind me to let You be my guide each day.

Remind me to tell someone else about Your way.

Remind me to think of those who have gone away.

Remind me to thank You for my family and friends who care.

Remind me of the blessings we all have to share.

A View From the Cross

What did Christ see looking down from the cross?
Did He see the people mourning, saying, "Oh what a loss"?
His thoughts—even to the very last—
Were of others and atoning for their past.

He saw the crowd milling around waiting for Him to die.
His only reaction was to pray for them to His father
    in the sky.
How He wanted to tell them, "Do not mourn,
For I will join you on that first Easter morn."

He knew from the beginning this had to be done.
He shed His blood for the sins of everyone.
He saw the mobs whose hearts were full of hate.

Could you have hung from the cross that day
And only have thought of others as you paused to pray?
The cross is empty now. We have nothing to fear.
He died for the sins of all He held so dear.

Lent

Crown of Thorns

A crown of thorns was placed on His blessed head.
An oath of scorn was the only prayer that was said.
He was held up for shame before they led Him away.
They had not listened to what He had to say.

They made Him haul His heavy load to the top of the hill.
It was a struggle, but He knew it was the way to pay our bill.
His suffering, His pain was all part of the Master's plan.
It was His way to get us to our Promised Land.

He did it all without having a single doubt,
For His Father in His wisdom had told Him what it was all about.
He arose from the grave so that we would not have to die.
Now He awaits us to come to our home in the sky.

Peace to All

Blessed peace in Jesus's love I have found.
No matter how I feel, it will never let me down.
It was purchased by Him on that Cross so long ago.
It calms my every fear wherever I may go.

This wondrous peace from a soul so divine.
His love seems much better with the passing of time.
It calms the winds that blow in a gale.
It comes from a love that's never been known to fail.
The peace I have found is a perfect delight.
It removes all fear and makes the dark clouds bright.

I searched the world over, but never have found
A peace that was paid for by wearing a thorny crown.
What a blessing the peace can give to all who believe.
It is so wonderful. It was fit for God to conceive.

Lent

We Won

It wasn't that He died on that cross on Friday.
It wasn't that He arose from that tomb on Sunday.
The blessing is that we all got a gift of love
That was sent to each of us from God above.

Jesus overcame the fear of death that day.
Now He shows us we can do the same by living His way.
Dying on the cross was an awful thing to have to do.
He did it to keep it from happening to me and you.

The way is easy and the cost is cheap,
For His promise to all He is sure to keep.

Lent

Always Easter

It all began in a very strange place.
The birth of the Savior of the human race.
The life He lived was not that of a king.
He was a messenger of love to every living thing.
There was trial after trial, as He went on His way.
But God was with Him. And nothing could lead Him astray.
They hung Him on a cross to satisfy an angry mob.
Even those who killed Him were among those who
    had to sob.

They put Him in a tomb and slowly went their way.
But He wasn't there when they came back on another day.
Many years have passed since He left that lonely grave.
He is in His heavenly home awaiting those He died to save.
The day of Easter proved that death we do not have to fear,
For he paid for our sins and we too will join the Savior
    so dear.

The Easter story grows better each year that we see,
For God's blessed son from our sins has set us free.
From Christmas to Easter, God's love has been there.
It's always present anytime or anywhere.

Easter

Christ Lives

Christ is alive and lives in our hearts each day.
We must let Him guide our thoughts and each word
    we have to say.

His life was hard, but He knew it would be from the very start.
He took the pain and denial, because our salvation
    was the only thing in His heart.
He died a shameful death on a cross between
    two sinful thieves.
He never refused, because He knew this was how
    His goal would be achieved.

But He still is active, working for all mankind's souls each day.
He needs us to help by spreading its meaning to everyone
    we meet on our way.
Christ is alive and still fights for our salvation by using
    people like you and me.
Christ is alive and will give us eternal life with God.
    And it's free.

Easter

Easter Every Day

May the love Christ showed for us that awful Friday
Be shared by each of us with others we meet every day.
God's grace should be told so everyone knows what
    it's all about.
Christ's life and death proved God's love beyond any doubt.

The love and grace that was shown that first Easter morning
Should fill our hearts and satisfy our every longing.
It starts when the Christ Child was born in all His glory,
And was fulfilled with His rebirth. Oh what a story.

With the Easter events fresh in our joyous hearts,
Reach out and urge others to get their fresh start.

Easter

Easter Grace

The cross is empty. So is the tomb. Christ is alive.
God has shown us to trust Him and we will survive.
His son bore the burden and felt all the pain.
He said, "Trust and follow Me, and you too will live again."

Our cost was nil. He paid for us all.
Just believe in His word. And answer His call.
The grace of God was shown for all of us to know.
And spread for everyone in every drop of blood that did flow.

The Easter glory that started with the miracle birth
Showed God's love for all of us who believe here on earth.

He Returned

Joy, joy, joy. Christ has returned from death to the earth.
Joy, joy, joy. This is His second birth.
Joy, joy, joy. He died that we might live.
Joy, joy, joy. What a gift He had to give.

Joy, joy, joy. This bright Easter Day.
Joy, joy, joy. He has taken our sins away.
Joy, joy, joy. He now lives that we will not die.
Joy, joy, joy. He will bring us to His home in the sky.

Joy, joy, joy. His suffering was not in vain.
Joy, joy, joy. The Savior lives once again.
Joy, joy, joy. The cross is empty now.
Joy, joy, joy. He has saved us with His power.

Joy, joy, joy. What glory this morning does bring.
Joy, joy, joy. Let us now sing as the angels did sing.
Joy, joy, joy. Let us sing, "Alleluia!" to our King.
Joy, joy, joy. What happiness this day does bring.
    Alleluia, Alleluia, Alleluia!

Easter

He Rose From the Tomb

He has arisen! What a beautiful thought.
His hard battle will not go for naught.
Like the thief on the cross, we will join Him someday.
He walked out of that tomb that glorious day.

After all the moaning and the tears that were shed,
Christ did arise even though He was dead.
He was born, lived, and died for each of us.
This was to let us enter heaven without a fuss.

The debt has been paid. We will join Him to pray.
He fulfilled His father's will that horrible Friday.
His time in the tomb was to set us free from sin.
Faith will make it possible as our journey we begin.

He has arisen! He has arisen! Let us shout it to all!
His kingdom has arrived, never to fall.
His path to the cross was hard to the end.
But now He will take us to His father as a friend.

The tomb could not hold Him. He knew all along,
So shout to the heavens His joyous song!
He lives! Let us thank God each day.
He lived just to take all our sins away.

Easter

His Rebirth Made It So

The cross is empty. The stone has been rolled away.

Our salvation has been assured by Christ on Easter Day.

We are His Easter people if he live by His plan.

He has paid for our home in Heaven for each
    woman and man.

The cross was awful and even harder to face.

But it was made easier for Him by God's loving grace.

We will face all our crosses as our lives go by.

They will all go away when we reach our home in the sky.

The debt has been paid. The deal has been made.

The sky may get cloudy, but God's love will not fade.

Easter

Welcome the Risen Lord

He has risen. Let us all welcome Him back like
 His father above.
He has atoned for our sins and waits for us with all
 His Godly love.

The cross is empty and so is the vault. They could not
 hold Him for long.
Let us welcome Him in our prayers and joyful song.

He lived among us to know our fears, our pains,
 and our sorrows.
By our faith in His promise, we will not feel them in
 heaven tomorrow.

Let us go forth telling those we meet of His love for all
 who believe in His word.
That He lives and is preparing a place where the love
 of God is all that is heard.

Yes, His cross is empty and by faith ours will be too.
Just believe in His love and the blood He shed for me and you.

Easter

The Graduate

Here's to the graduate! May he stand tall.
May his search for knowledge never take a fall.
May the hours spent studying books cover to cover
Now help what he has learned lead him to reach out
    to others.
The lessons he learned that led him to this day.
The prayers that were answered every sort of way.

Stride down that aisle with a grace so proud.
Shake that hand and say, "Thank you," with a voice so loud.
It was all the labor he did to make this dream come true.
It was his determination that did see him through.
Sometimes he thought, *I can't do all of this,*
But with that diploma in his hand, what bliss.

Life isn't over but has just begun.
He has learned that he can do anything under the sun.

Special Times

Valentine Wish

Happy Valentine's Day we wish to each other once a year.
But it should be wished every day to show we care.

It tells all we greet just how much they are in our love.
Just another way of mirroring God's love from above.

So "Happy Valentine's Day with all our love," I say to everyone.
This is from our hearts and is not just a pun.

We Must Follow

Spring is here and the cold earth has come to life.
Christ has risen and settled all the strife.
The cross is empty, and sin's debts have been paid.
The tomb is empty where once His body had been laid.

All this happened because of God's love and grace.
The Son came to earth to save the human race.
Our sins were atoned for but with a lot of pain.
There is nothing to lose but eternal life to gain.

Christ paid the price on the cross that day.
All we must do is trust and live in His way.
No one else has ever shown that kind of love.
It was designed to bring us to our home above.

God knew we would not change and turn from sin.
It's only by faith in His grace that we will be allowed in.

Special Times

Sympathy

A Lonely Child's Prayer

I heard a child the other day
As beside his bed he knelt to pray.
"Oh Lord, I ask for nothing with which to play.
All I want next Christmas Day
Is my father who has gone far away.
He left one morning when the sun shone bright.
He told my mother that for us, he was going to fight."

One day a messenger boy came by.
Mom read the letter and began to cry.
Oh why, Lord, did it have to be?
A guy who loved his country like he.
No, he didn't mind his life to give
So others might have the right to live.

That was the prayer I heard that day.
So let us not let this prayer go astray.
His father died just a few years ago.
But many people have forgotten G.I. Joe.
So many of our young have gone this day.
Let us all pray that it ends someday.

No Chance to Say Good-Bye

Without a chance to say good-bye, they were gone
    to their home in the sky.
We will never know the reason, for only God really knows why.

What can we say that has not been told?

Their zest for life put us all to the test.
Whatever they did, they gave it their best.
Their caring love they gave to all they met.
And where they are now, they are doing it yet.

Their joy in life was to care for others,
For to them we were all their sisters and brothers.
We all must tread the path they have trod.
Now they are with their Savior and God.

The pleasures they gave to all in their years
Cannot be washed away by the shedding of tears.
Their lives on earth were a gift from God.
And they took His word with them wherever they trod.

Let's not mourn them, but give thanks to our Lord,
Knowing someday we will meet them in that heavenly horde.
God in His wisdom let us share them for awhile.
Now those in His kingdom will share their loving smiles.

In Memory of Him

Why are we mourning? We should rejoice.
He lived a full life. He always made the choice.
His love for his family, country, and God, you could see.
His service to all is the way it had to be.

The voice he was given he shared with us all.
He loved to sing anytime: winter, spring, summer, or fall.
The stories he told we looked forward to with glee.
The happiness in his face you could always see.

He is much happier in his home above
Where he will be waiting for his true love.
He traveled the world wherever he was sent.
His love for his fellowman never relented.

We will not say good-bye, but so long for awhile.
For someday we will meet him and his friendly smile.

He will be missed and that's putting it lightly,
But know that he is with his Lord Almighty.
Do not grieve him, but shout with glee.
For he has gone home to wait for you and me.

So Long

The time has come and I must go.
I'm not ready, but the Lord said so.
He went ahead, so everything is set.
The cost was great, but He has paid the debt.
We know not the hour or even the day.
When He is ready, He will have His say.

The life I had here was as good as could be.
Now the rewards that await I will soon see.
To those I loved here on this good earth,
It's not a good-bye but my new birth.
He has prepared a place for each of us there.
For all eternity I will exist there without a care.

Do not mourn, for there is no room for tears there.
For God's love has replaced our every care.
My life was a blessing. And all has been made right.
Now I will await you from my heavenly site.
So long now. And do not shed even one little tear.
For I go knowing that with love there is no fear.

Sorrow Will Go

When someone you love is taken away,
No one knows just the right thing to say.

Only God knows when or even why.
But even His son for our sins had to die.
When we are born, no one knows how long we will live.
Jesus came and died. This was the gift He came to give.

Sorrow is hard, but time will ease the pain.
Through God's love and our faith, we will meet again.
They have walked the path we all must tread.
With our faith, we know a life in God's love is ahead.

Throughout His life, Jesus's message was always the same.
Trust in Him. And eternal life will be what we gain.

Thanks to An Angel

One of God's angels has gone to his rest.
Whatever he did he did with his very best.
Wherever he was called, he was willing to go.
His message was simple: "God loves you so."

The smile on his face was a sure giveaway.
He knew for a fact it was true what he had to say.

Let's not moan but be glad that he was with us for awhile.
For wherever he went, he was serving the Christ Child.

Let's thank God He let us share him this long.
We know he will be welcomed in heaven with a song.
His faith was strong, and he trusted in God's grace.
Now his reward will be he will meet Him face-to-face.

So Long for Awhile

Without a chance to say good-bye, he was gone to his home
    in the sky.
We will never know the reason, for only God really knows why.

What can we say that has not been told?

His zest for life put us all to the test.
Whatever he did, he gave it his best.
His caring love he gave to all he met.
And where he is now, he is doing it yet.

His joy in life was to care for others,
For to him we were all his sisters and brothers.
We all must tread the path he has trod.
Now he is with his Savior and God.

The pleasures he gave to all in his years
Cannot be washed away by the shedding of tears.
His life on earth was a gift from God.
And he took His word with him wherever he trod.

Let's not mourn him, but give thanks to our Lord,
Knowing someday we will meet him in that heavenly horde.
God in his wisdom let us share him for awhile.
Now those in His kingdom will share his loving smile.

Trust

A Dream

I dreamed the other night I was at the Master's knee.
During the talk He said, "I died on the cross so this could be."
He told of His kingdom that is to come
Where love fills the thoughts of everyone.
He said everything would go smoothly there.
That life would go on each day and everyone His love
    would share.

Oh, what a joyous time that will be
When only loving and caring are all we see.

This was His teaching everywhere on Earth He went:
Stop all the greed and hate. Just repent.
He told us of our perfect home above.
That it could be reached only by love.

Trust in Him. He has done the rest.
Live your life for only the best.

Always With Us

God has promised to be with us wherever we go,
So we need to step out in His name, because we know it is so.
He gave His message to the prophets many years ago.
They faced their enemies and told them
God wanted them to let His people go.

We never take a step without His knowledge.
He goes with us to our work or to our college.
He is with us every breath that we take.
He sent His son to pay for our every mistake.

We should never feel lonely. He is always there.
Just listen, and He will tell us when answering our prayer.
If we go in His name, we have nothing to fear.
We don't go anywhere that He is not near.
From the bottom of the ocean to the highest place,
God has promised to be with us with His love and grace.

Get Closer to God

Get closer to God. He wants you to hear Him.
Answer His call. Don't be like others and be left out on a limb.
He calls you in many ways, but so many never answer His call.
Listen for Him whether you are in bed or on stage
    in a great hall.

He loves you so much He sent His son to die for your sin.
Share His love to all you meet: stranger, neighbor, or kin.

The closer you get to Him, the more you will learn that
    His love is true.
Take His hand when you're in trouble, and He
    will see you through.
Without living your life holding His hand, your life is in vain.
With Him near to you, He will always ease even
    the smallest pain.

Good Shepherd

Little Bo Peep lost her sheep and so has our Lord, it seems.
But with the love of us and the Holy Spirit, those lost
    can find their dreams.

Around God's earth many people go to bed hungry
    because they have nothing to eat.
If we all would share a little of their hunger pains,
    their hunger could be beat.

Even though the world around us is filled with evil and sin,
If we stray, God's love will bring us back home.
    He will let us in.

When you are born, you spend a lot of time in your
    mother's arms.
When you reach life's end, you will be welcomed into
    God's arms without any qualms.

We live in a world where temptation is placed before
    our every turn.
Just stay close to our Savior, and He will teach us
    His way to learn.

The Lord is our shepherd and He will lead us every day.
Believe in Him and He will never lead you astray.

He Held Me

He hugged me. He reached out and hugged me.
I was feeling low, but He made me see.
With his arms He held me so tight.
He gave me strength to see me through the night.

Now I know that I have nothing to fear.
I can call on Him because He is always near.
No matter the doubt I might feel,
I know His love for me is always real.
Wherever I roam, however I stray,
I can always come back to His arms to stay.

His love lifts me up and sets me free.
I know this is always the way it will be.
His arms are a shelter from whatever I face.
These things are possible because of His grace.

I Am Here

From the mountaintops to the shores,
God is inviting us to come like never before.
The birds that soar in the sky above us.
They live and feed without a fuss.
The sun rises each morning to bring us a new day.
God in His wisdom has made it this way.
The flowers they bloom in the same way,
As if to say, "Look what God has given you today."

People are crying and some are upset.
But if they turn to God, their happiness they will get.
It's up to us all to spread the good news
That love and contentment will offset the blues.
Just open your eyes and look all around:
God isn't lost, because His love can always be found.
God shouts from everything He has made,
"I'm here, I'm here, and My love will never fade."

In His Loving Arms

When the winds get high and the waves get tall,
Trust you will be in His arms.
When the sky is blue and the sun shines brightly,
Trust you are still in His arms.

When your plan seems to go bad,
Just trust, for you are still in His arms.
When your heart is filled with joy and everything is right,
It's because you are in His arms.

When you feel that everything seems to go wrong,
Have no fear. You are in His arms.
When you awake with a smile and feel so well,
It's because you have been asleep in His arms.

When you feel like Job and think that God has forgotten,
Don't despair. You are in His arms.
Morning or night. Good times or bad.
With faith, you are in His arms.

Trust

Nothing's Impossible

As He calmed the waves on the Sea of Galilee,
He can calm the storms for you and me.
We cannot limit the peace His love can bring.
It is always there for every living thing.

His power isn't limited into making water into wine.
He has showered His love on all of mankind.
He walked on water and raised those who were dead.
If we listen to His words, we know what lies ahead.

He lived on earth and died for all our sins.
His love was for all and will have no end.
He fed the crowd with food blessed from above.
His message was that everything is solved with God's love.

Wherever He went, His message was always the same:
God's love is for all and will not lead to shame.
Whatever the problem in life you are called to face,
Put your faith in God and trust in His loving grace.

Praise God Alone

Each day, we should go to God in prayers of thanksgiving
    and direction for the day,
Then stop and listen for every word and thought He
    will send our way.
The Bible teaches—from cover to cover—that there is only
    one true God,
And He loves us all.
When man started to stray from God's ways,
He sent another leader to keep them on the ball.

We are living in a different age filled with all kinds of gods:
Money, power, and all kinds of sin.
But as Moses taught His people and Christ taught
    His followers,
There is only one God from start to end.

So we must take care that there is nothing taking precedence
Over our love for our Lord.
We must never let our love for other things be put
    ahead of God,
Or we will be part of the sinful horde.

"There shall be no other gods before Me." That
    means everyone.
So we must go out each day and spread the word of God
    and His son.

Reach for Him

God's love shines the brightest when life's clouds
    are the darkest.
His love is the greatest when our spirits are the lowest.
Reach for His hand when you need someone to hold you.
He is always there with a support that is forever true.

Your day will be better if you speak to Him first.
He's always ready to satisfy your every need or thirst.
Should you start to fall, His arms are there to pull you
    to His side.
You may stray from His way, but from His love you
    can never hide.

God's love is everywhere and big enough for all to share.
Nothing is too hard for Him to handle and say, "Yes, I care."
God's love is available, so reach out for His nail-scarred hands.
Hold them tightly and He will take you home to
    His promised land.

Stories of Inspiration

A Mission to Do
Ezekiel 2:3

God spoke to Ezekiel and gave him a job to do. As it was with most of the prophets in the Old Testament, his job—like the jobs of the others—was to turn God's chosen people away from their evil ways and back to their faith in the one true God. This had been a constant battle. Abraham faced it when God told him he would be the father of a great nation.

The easier God made life for His people, the more they wanted to stray from His ways. They would accept other people's ways and turn away from God's teachings.

Like Ezekiel, our mission is to bring people back to His ways. Though God did not cause us to fall down in awe, in His own way, He has touched each of us and has urged us to bring people back to their faith.

In olden times, God used fear to enforce His laws, but Jesus changed that to love.

Jesus taught that we should love each other as He had loved us. His love was so great that He gave His life to pay for the sins He knew we would commit. Yes, our slate has been washed clean, free from sin. All we have to do is believe in Him, have faith, and share that faith with others so they too can come to Him.

As one of the old hymns said, "Love lifted me." Let this same love lift you out of this sinful world and return you back to a faith founded on faith and love.

Just think what a faith it must have been that kept Jesus on His path to the cross on His mission that was given to Him by His Father.

Let's all hope we too can fulfill our mission.

Out-Giving God

For many years, I have fought the battle with myself about being a good steward. I have lived my life in and around the church, straying away but always returning. I have learned that stewardship and faith in God go hand in hand. The more our faith grows, the more our stewardship concerns grow.

In the last few years, I have come to one conclusion. There is only one impossible thing. You cannot out-give God. He has given you everything. Are you willing to do the same?

Looking back over my life, I can see His gifts that I never recognized. There are so many I cannot list them all. I'm trying to highlight a few.

Once our pastor was trying to raise money to get a family into their home. He asked me for $5.00. I only had a $20 bill, and he had no change. I told him to take the 20, because my bills were paid. A few days later, a dividend check arrived in the mail. It usually was for $30.00, but this time it was for $80.00.

I have had to buy pills for my sick child when I didn't have the money. I dropped off the prescription and went home. And there was a check from someone for more than I needed to pay the drug bill.

When my in-laws were forced to retire in New York City, they needed better living conditions. We found a home with separate quarters for them. When we purchased it, we had to have a second mortgage as part of the down payment in order to take over a low-interest loan. I was to pay the first note; then they were to pay the second note. One month after paying off the second note, my father-in-law died, leaving his wife with no income. But I could take care of payments then.

These are just three times when I felt that God had provided the way for me to pay.

My first encounter at pledging for a church budget came when we started a mission Lutheran church. I couldn't see how we could pledge much on our income. We made our commitment and kept it up for a year. That was my first exposure to a stewardship drive. We had a person come and tell us how we could give more. There was the talk of tithing, but I thought we could never do that. Within the year, we had attained the goal of tithing and had just as much as before.

Then came the Building Fund Drive and more needs. After much prayer and discussion, I increased my giving to over 10% of my income. The next day on the job, my boss called me in and told me I would receive a raise the next week, which dropped me back to 10% of my income.

Over my working life, this happened on many occasions. I do not believe that you can buy favors from God, but I strongly believe He will provide for you if you will only give Him the credit and don't think that you are the one who controls things. I can honestly say that over the last 40 years, I have not made a major decision financially or otherwise without first taking it to the Lord in faithful prayer. Then I never worry about it. I believe He will take care of it.

God makes no plea bargains. But believe and trust in Him, and He will solve all problems. Not always to your liking. He didn't promise that. But always for your betterment. He said that we should pick up our cross and follow His way.

As a naval chaplain told all of us sailors, "Don't do as I do, but do as I tell you."

Christ instructed us to follow in His footsteps. Thank God that He is there when we stray, to forgive us.

Stewardship Thought

November is always a hard month in each year. We are reaching the end of another church year. We must prepare for the coming year and its unknown needs.

As in each of our lives, the church's life is filled with unknowns. The only sure thing in life is God's love. Everything else is subject to change: the seasons, the weather, and our lives. In this mobile society we live in, we live here today, but may be living somewhere else next week. Again the only sure thing is God's love.

Each year we must face the most-feared word in the church's discussion: *stewardship*. This word seems to be feared more than any other one. Most people don't like to face the fact that it takes many dollars to maintain and run the church. Our church leaders must have an idea what to expect so they can set up plans for the coming year. This has been true for years.

In Deuteronomy 15:10, we read "For the Lord will prosper you in everything you do." And in Deuteronomy 16:17 it says "Give as you are able, according as the Lord has blessed you." While the prophets were talking to a people just out of slavery in Egypt in these Deuteronomy passages, these are very true even in this day and time.

Each day we should take a few moments to think of all of the blessings God gives us. When we think of all these things, we should look forward to saying, "Yes, Lord, I will do my share." Over the years you will find that—like your faith—your support for the church will grow as God has promised. He has never failed to provide for His people.

Make a list of your blessings. I know that every day you will add to this list. When the time comes to make your commitment, how will you support the church's programs in the coming year?

Always remember that God's love is the only sure thing.

The Golden Rule

As a child I was taught and lived by a different version of the Golden Rule. At an early age I remember my grandfather telling me, "Don't ever ask anyone to do anything for you that you are not willing to do for them." I still try to live by this rule.

Throughout His ministry, Christ taught us to love one another. He could have escaped the cross. But because of His love for others, He died only to live again. What a true love. He died so we would not have to pay for our sins.

Down through the ages, the Golden Rule has been the foundation for most civil laws. Treat each other as you want to be treated.

Somewhere this basic rule has changed over the years until now the basic rule is to do unto others before they do it to you.

The respect we have been taught is being eroded away. Now our nature is to doubt what we are told. If we don't like what we are told, we look for another view until we find what we want.

Somehow we must turn this trend around. We must learn to trust and live with our fellowman. This can only happen when we all learn to live by the basic rule.

"Do unto others as you would have them do unto you." Let's try it.

Time to Serve

When we watch television, we see someone telling us what they think is for our benefit. It might be an ad for some product or service or organization that they want us to support. They all say it's best for us.

We watch a parade and see people trying to influence our thoughts. We see everything from various branches of the military to the bands from all kinds of schools. Whatever each group may be, they all plead for our support.

We drive down the street and see signs wanting us to try new things.

As a Christian, have you ever asked yourself, *Why aren't we out there with floats in the parade and with signs on the street that state our beliefs?*

When was the last time you talked to anyone about your faith, be it a stranger or a family member? People who belong to civic organizations don't hesitate to ask for our support. They ring bells to get coins in a pot. They sell flowers, cookies, magazines, and candy, always in support of a cause that they believe in.

We see signs on T-shirts, jackets, and caps showing the support for a favorite team or school. Wearers do so with pride because they believe.

We see both men and women wearing pins in support of our country or other things. But we see few such pins that support prayer, which is our basic foundation.

Let's face it for what it is. Christians are a target for everything, and it is time for us to start to fight for what we believe in. Wear the sign of the cross, and tell everyone how and why you believe. Invite them to worship with you. Don't be ashamed of your faith.

We are at war every day with the devil and must fight him with every means we can. Say to everyone, "This is what I believe and how I live." Yes, pick up your cross and follow Him. He has told us how to be His followers. He led the way. Now it's up to us to act. We must be His messengers.

Christ needs more soldiers to win His war on Satan. Won't you enlist today? Just say, "Yes, Lord, send me."

Walking on Water

The other day we heard the story of Jesus walking on water. I think this is one of my favorite parts of the Bible.

Jesus came to His disciples, who were out in a boat fishing and got caught in a storm. All of a sudden here came Jesus walking across the water toward them.

When Peter saw whom it was, he said, "If You tell me to, I can come to You on the water." So Jesus said, "Come." Peter stepped out of the boat and walked toward Jesus. His faith was so strong that he knew he could do it.

Then all of a sudden he took his eyes off Jesus and started to sink because his thoughts were not centered on Jesus but on himself. We can do *anything* if Jesus is at its center. Everything we do must be for the advancement of His kingdom.

We go through life knowing Jesus but not putting our total trust in Him. We want to be in control of what we do in life, but this is not possible because for most of our lives we must trust in our faith in Jesus. I believe that it would be possible for each of us to walk across the water if our faith were as strong as Peter's was when he first spoke to Jesus. But like Peter, little doubts set in. All we can do is to trust in His word and live as He has taught us.

Jesus's entire life was given in love for His fellowman so we could spend eternity with Him. Doubt should never enter our minds. He paid the price for each of us, if only we would put our faith in Him.

Like Peter when he was asked by Jesus, "Whom do you say I am?", our reply should always be, "Our Lord and Savior."

What's He Telling Us?

Every day for over a month the radio, TV, and newspapers have been filled with stories about the storms hitting the Gulf Coast and what havoc they have done to the area.

The strange thing that happened at the same time the first storm hit was that our Bible passage for that Sunday was about Jonah being sent to Nineveh to deliver God's message to the people there to change their ways. Jonah told them that they had to return to their belief in His teachings or that God was going to destroy them. After much preaching by Jonah, the people did listen, repented, and returned to following His word, so many lives were saved.

Every week we hear of major storms, fires, and earthquakes happening all over our world. Could these be messages to everyone? Change your ways and turn back to a life led by God's word.

Each Sunday there are plenty of empty seats in many churches, because so many people have other things to do instead of going to hear the word of God.

We live in an evil world most of the week, so we need to be with fellow Christians once a week to get renewed strength for another week of fighting Satan. It's like taking your car and filling the tank so it can take you a little farther down the road. We need that extra help to keep telling people what Christ can do for them.

Though the storm clouds pass over, with our faith in Him we know He will take care of us in His own way. Our faith will see us through each day. Or He will take us home to be with Him.

When I read the Bible, I am amazed at the times God uses natural disasters or nonbelieving nations to harm His people to bring them back to a stronger faith in Him. How would we react?

What's in It for Me?

The other day as I walked by the TV, I heard someone say, "What's in it for me?"

I had heard and said this statement many times. Although I didn't know the background for this having been said, it started me thinking about what it really meant.

What if Jesus had said it when He was tempted by the devil in the wilderness? He still would have ruled the world that would have been controlled by the devil, not by His loving Father. Surely that would have changed all our lives. Sometimes we have doubts, but His love finally wins out.

What if He had asked this at the wedding feast when he changed water into wine? This—the first of His many miracles that affected so many lives for the worse. Jesus didn't gain a thing.

What if He had asked this of the blind man before He gave the man his sight? That man had nothing to offer, but he did have faith to do as he was told.

What if He had thought this when he learned of the death of Lazarus? Jesus gained nothing. But He gave a brother back to his two sisters who had first loved him.

What if He had come down from that cross as He was urged to do by the two thieves? Yes, He could have lived. But how we would have suffered.

Yes, His life was lived in service to others. But never once did He ask, "What's in it for me?"

He came to this world to atone for our sins. Yes, He died on that cross for you and me. Never in His entire ministry—though He was abused, insulted, spat upon, and killed—did He once ask His father, "What's in it for me?" He lived so that God's will could be done.

Each time you pick up your Bible, you should know what's in it for you. When you accepted Jesus as your Savior and when you live by His word, you know what's in it for you.

Who Is Calling You?
I Samuel—Chapter 3

At an early age, Samuel worked in the temple as an aide to Eli, the priest, who was almost blind and very old.

One night Samuel was awakened by Eli calling his name. This happened several times. Each time Samuel went to Eli, but it wasn't Eli who was calling. Samuel finally realized it was God who was calling him. He listened carefully to what God had to say, and his life was changed.

Have you ever thought about how many times God may have called you to do something and you disregarded this call?

How many times have we heard people within our church ask for help for a project to help out our fellowman? Could this be one of God's ways to call us?

Every other month our church goes to Weaver House to feed the needy. Have you ever thought that this could be what He wants you to do?

We never know what our words or actions will do for others. We are taught in the Bible that we cannot do all things but that we can be a part of the whole thing.

The next time you hear of a job that needs to be done, ask yourself if you could be a part of this work.

Samuel was called by God, but it took him a while to hear Him. The next time you think it may be God calling you, just reply and ask Him to use you.

Every time we pray we should ask Him for His guidance. Then we should look for Him to lead us.

Jesus called His disciples one at a time. If we listen He will call us.

From the beginning to the end, the Bible is full of stories in which God used ordinary people to fulfill His plans for mankind. Who knows whom He will call next? I knew a man who was an executive with Ford Motor Company. He left it all to go into the ministry at age 55.

Stop, look, and listen.

Without Love
I Corinthians 13:13

You pick up the newspaper or watch TV, and almost all you can see are people hating other people for one reason or another.

What has happened to the love that God has given to all people? For years we have sung a song that said, "Love makes the world go round." If we don't soon find a way to spread that God-given love to others, man and his superego will find a way to destroy this wonderful planet that our God has given us to live on.

Throughout the Bible we read of God's love for man and His acts to show people how to love others.

During our entire lives, we are told that we have three things to live by: faith, hope, and love. We are told that the greatest of these is love.

Daily we watch many ways that man is so eager to show his anger against his fellowman. But this must change in some way. We must turn our faith back to a trust in God and in His wisdom. We must turn away from all of the other things that tend to lead to hate and distrust.

In the last year or so, I have noticed many youngsters attending our worship services. Each of us should be trying to find a way to keep them interested in what God is doing for them. Parents can bring them, but everyone else should show them God's love.

Each week we are taught that God has chosen us for His followers. But it is up to us to say yes and then to act on our commitment. He made the call. But will we accept His call and pass it on to someone else?

People are always looking for a better life. Everyone needs love, so let's try to spread that love of God to someone else each day. Find the peace that God's love will bring, and give it to someone else.

What a wonderful place this would be if we only knew love as God does.

Your Choice
Genesis 4:7

"You will be accepted if you respond in the right way. But if you refuse to respond right, then watch out! Sin is waiting to attack you and destroy you, and you must subdue it."

Everyone was born with a choice. We can follow the path we want to choose, but we must pay for the wrong choice.

God has called each of us. It is our choice to listen and answer this call. Since the time of Adam, we have all been given that choice. Adam paid dearly for his choice not to follow what God had told him. All people who have come after Adam are still paying the price.

Each day when we awake, we start to make choices. Do we turn over and stay in bed awhile, or do we get started? We must get up and start another day. That is the choice that our boss controls. Every minute of each day we are making choices, never knowing how many lives each choice will affect.

We do not choose our parents. That was decided by God. We do not choose our relatives. That also was decided years ago by God. We did have the choice of telling them about our love for them and for Jesus. We also had the choice of telling them why we choose to accept Christ as our Lord and Savior.

Every time we choose to tell someone about our love for God, the stronger our faith will get.

With every choice we make, we should ask ourselves, *What would Jesus do?* Then we should follow the feeling in our hearts.

Don't go through life without making the right choice. Make it now. Go to God in prayer and tell Him, "Lord, here is my life. Use it to advance Your kingdom." He is calling you every day. What better time is there to answer His call than at the beginning of a new year? What could be better? A new life and a new year.

A Cross and the Easter Season

"For the preaching of the cross is to them that perish foolishness; but unto us which are saved it is the power of God."
—I Corinthians 1:18

On a table in my living room is a small glass cross with beveled edges, behind which stands a mirror. In between them is a small candle burning. When you look at this from any angle, the cross seems to go on forever.

Whenever I walk through the living room or even sit in my recliner, it reminds me of Christ coming to be the Light of the World. And the cross goes on forever.

As we approach this Easter season, we will hear and think more about the cross and what it means to us.

Even though the secular world has tried to make it into something else, for those of us who believe in Jesus, we can see Easter for what it was meant to be. It is the answer to why Christ came to earth on that joyous day that we celebrate as Christmas. Yes, He came for one purpose, and that was to atone for our sins. Yes, by believing in His promise and trusting in His words, we are assured of our place in His kingdom someday. Yes, it was an awful way to die, but he suffered through it for each of us.

It is my earnest prayer that each time you see a cross, you will remember it as a sign of what He went through for each of us. Take time to give a prayer of thanks.

Yes, Easter is a joyous occasion and a call for celebration. But let us also remember what its true cause for celebration is: our eternal life paid for by His death on that cross.

Abundant Love

"I have come that they may have life, and have it more abundantly."—John 10:10

Several years ago I heard a speaker say that everyone's heart has a throne and a cross. When man is on the throne and Christ is on the cross, things are not right. The question is, "Where is Christ in each of our hearts?" Our lives will not be complete until Christ comes down off the cross and sits on the throne in each of our hearts, there to rule each of our lives.

This is what we face each day at work, at home, and on the road. He must guide our every encounter and how we handle it. We never make a decision that does not affect someone's life. The smiles on our faces and the sounds of our voices demonstrate that. Everything we do reflects how Christ affects our lives.

In His ministry, He served everyone: the rich and the poor, the believer and those who did not believe. Wherever He went and whatever He did, His every action was to show His love for all. Whether it was making wine from water, curing the sick, or raising the dead, it was always to help someone else. He told everyone involved in each situation that it was their faith that made the outcome possible.

Christ taught that "He came to earth so we could have life and have it more abundantly." Let us live so that Christ is always on the throne ruling our lives, because it is our faith in Him that will see us through each day. He is always there; just let Him take over.

Christmas Is a Promise Kept
Isaiah 40:10-11

We have just been through another Christmas season. The beginning of the Christian faith. In a lowly manger in a desolate part of our world, our God came to earth in the form of a small baby boy. He was born to live and die for the atonement of our sins. Thus He fulfilled His promise that He would be with us always.

Year after year, humans try to erode the true meaning of Christ's birth, but we truly accept by faith what our forefathers have told us happened. It can only be God's way of keeping His promise when He chose the people of Israel as His people.

His birth was the start. His life and teachings were the way. His death and rebirth were the proof that He was whom we proclaim Him to be.

Our salvation cannot be purchased. It cannot be earned by what we do. It comes only by faith.

Let's all start the new year with our hearts longing to be strong believers with a commitment to spreading His teachings to all those we meet in our daily lives. Remember: each time you share your faith, the stronger it becomes.

For beginning a new year, it is always best to review your past mistakes and strive to go forth with a new vigor to live a better life in Christ.

God always keeps His promises. Let us each try to keep ours and worship Him every chance we get and live each day as He has taught us.

Hope to see you in church on Sunday.

Come to Me

"Come to me, all you who labor and are heavy laden, and I will give you rest. Take My yoke upon you and learn from Me, for I am gentle and lowly in My heart, and you will find rest for your souls. For My yoke is easy and My burden is light."—Matthew 11:28-30

I remember as a child sitting in church and singing a hymn that said, "Take your burdens to the Lord and leave them there." How many times have we tried to do that? Why is it that we believe we have taken our burdens to Him only to bring them back with us again?

So many times I have taken my burdens to Him, only to bring them back to me. I don't know if it was my pride or my lack of faith that caused me to do this. I don't know when or why it came to me that if I truly had the faith in Him that I claim I have, I should take Him at His word. Ever since I came to realize this, I have saved myself many a worry.

Another old hymn comes to mind: "Trust and Obey." Though it's hard to do, it is the only way to find perfect peace.

Endangered
Psalm 12:1

Every so often we hear of some kind of life-form becoming endangered in its existence. In studying ancient history, we have read about different animals like the dodo bird and other types of life that have just disappeared.

In this psalm David is crying to God for help since he believes that His people have lost their faith in the true God and are turning to other things to worship.

Throughout the Old Testament, the prophets had to battle to keep their people living by their faith in God. God in His wisdom realized that this would be hard, so He sent His son to show people the way. When we accept Jesus as our Savior and put our complete trust in Him, He has paid the debts for our sins and has set us free of our guilt. But it takes total surrender. The human ego doesn't accept this dependence well.

We want to be in charge. We want to change God's plan to fit what we want to do. We, too, will become endangered without this total acceptance of Jesus. He said, "I am the way." This means He must be our guide in everything we do. Not only should we live this way, but we also should pass it on to all we are in contact with. We should live it every day in every way. If we don't pass it on to the next generation, we too will be on the endangered list.

Always ask yourself, "Is this what God would have me do?" Then listen for His answer when you pray. Will the Christian way of life be like the dodo bird? It will if we don't pass our faith on to others. Share faith with everyone. The more you share it, the more it will mean to you. What a beautiful place earth would be if everything were ruled by the Golden Rule.

Follow Jesus. Let Him lead the way.

God's Gift

"And she gave birth to her firstborn son and wrapped Him in bands of cloth, and laid Him in a manger, because there was no place for them in the inn."—Luke 2:7

He was born in a stable and His bed was a manger. He was a gift from God so we all might live. From this meager beginning came a life so great it changed all of history and has changed many lives ever since. His coming was foretold by prophets of old. His birth was announced by bands of angels. He was welcomed to earth by Wise Men of His age who were led by a star. Born a king, He still reigns today. But from the beginning there were those who sought to do Him harm.

Each year His birthday is celebrated by billions of people on December 25 in many different ways. For those who believe in Him, it is a day to give thanks and joy for God's great gift to mankind. We do this by giving gifts to those around us. Even those who do not believe in Him seem to try to show love for their fellowman.

This year—as in so many years in the past—many military people will be in a faraway land serving their country. Be sure to remember them in your celebration. Pray for their safe return.

As this holiday season approaches, I can think of no better way to honor Him than to reach out and tell someone what His birth has meant to you.

As you spread your joy with others, keep in mind that Wise Men Still Seek Him. Maybe you will be the one who leads others to Him.

Let us all live so that every day is a Christ Must Day.

Gone Fishing

"As Jesus walked beside the Sea of Galilee, He saw Simon and his brother Andrew casting a net into the lake, for they were fishermen. 'Come; follow me,' Jesus said, 'and I will make you fishers of men.' "—Mark 1:16-17

A few weeks ago—printed on the back of the offering envelope in large letters—were the words "Gone Fishing" and a little reminder that the church expenses go on whether we are fishing or swimming.

When Christ was gathering His disciples, He told some of them to put away their nets and come with Him. He would make them fishers of men. And so off they went.

When we became Christians, we too became fishers of men. In the early years of the church, Christ's followers would identify themselves by drawing fish signs in the dirt. While I can't think of a more-relaxing time or way to spend a few hours than on or beside a lake, we as followers of Christ should always be fishing for new followers of Christ. You never know which kind word or loving act might be the one that changes a life. I cannot think of a greater reward than to say I am the one who brought someone to Christ.

Remember: the more you give your faith away, the stronger it becomes. So come on. Cast your line out and see whom you reel in!

Have You Met Life Today?

"In everything do to others as you would have them do to you; for this is the law of the prophets."—Matthew 7:12

Several weeks ago while watching a football game on TV, a blimp flew over the crowd of about 80,000 people. On its side was printed "HAVE YOU MET LIFE TODAY?" It made me stop and think about just what it was asking.

How many people in the crowd had really thought about their life before they started out that morning? Some had stopped to thank God for another day, but most had probably set out with only the game on their minds. They had thought that everything else could wait until tomorrow. Only tomorrow never gets here, because it is always today.

Jesus taught that we should always do unto others as we want to be treated and that we should live our lives, never putting off till later anything that could be done today. I know I am the worst at putting things off.

I once read this statement in a book: "I cannot give anything without getting something for it." Over my years I have found this to be true, especially with my faith. The more I have shared it, the stronger it gets.

Try sharing your faith with someone, and see how much more it means to you. Count your blessings; then share them with someone else. The Pilgrims did this with their first harvest, and each year we still do this.

Use the many gifts God has given you to help others see what He has given them.

Live today, for there is no tomorrow.

He Is Always There

"For this world in its present form is passing away."
—I Corinthians 7:31

In the last few weeks we have been reminded that our world and our lives are in a constant mode of change. Almost every day we hear of a storm, an earthquake, or other disasters that have caused changes. Each day we live, our bodies change. We feel another ache or pain. These are the things we must be prepared to meet.

We awake each morning never thinking that some disaster will strike. We go on our way without fear. Life is a lot easier to face when we know we are protected by our faith in Christ. He has given us the way to eternal life. Through baptism He has given us this freedom. As an old hymn says, "Trust and obey, for there is no other way." It is this trust that lets us face life each day, not knowing what the day might bring.

It is the knowledge that He died to atone for our sins. Yes, it is our faith that makes our life worth living. Yes, our lives and our world are changing each day, but it is only our faith in God's word that lets us look forward to meeting these changes.

Christ has been with us always.

Investment

"For where your treasure is, there your heart will be also."
—Matthew 6:21

The other day as I listened to a motivational speaker talk, it got me thinking. I have worked all my life, and what have I got to show for it? No stocks, no bonds, no big estate, or bank accounts.

I invested in my family and my church.

My family has paid wonderful dividends. They all grew up to be good people with a love for God, and they have children of their own. In times of sorrow, they are always there. What more could you want?

Through my church, I have stayed in touch with my God and with tithing. I feel that I am returning a part of what He has first given me. When you honestly look at it, it belongs to Him anyway.

I have heard about people who invested a few dollars and ended up making millions. I think my investment came years ago when a young man I knew made a decision to go into the ministry. With the help of his family and part-time jobs, he finished his four years of college. But when it came time for him to enter the seminary, his family couldn't help. A group of men from our church decided we would give the financial help he needed.

When he finished his schooling, this young new pastor took a job in which he would develop a church on the outskirts of Atlanta, Georgia. From this mission came one of the largest Lutheran churches in the area. Now he is working with the Southeast Synod teaching other churches how to reach out.

Looking at the support we gave him as an investment, I would say that our investment paid a very good return. Just think of the many lives and churches our investment has changed. Don't we wish that all we invest in could turn out this way?

Lip Service

"These people honor Me with their lips, but their hearts are far away."—Mark 2:7

As we spend our busy lives, we read and see people who are at many points in their lives. When I read this Bible verse, it caused me to wonder how it applied to my life. How did I need to change?

We go to the altar for communion, but do we realize what an awful price Jesus had to pay for us to truly receive this forgiveness? Do we leave that altar with a sense of true forgiveness, or are we still leaded with that heavy burden of sin? Yes, He paid for our sin and died for us. We should all leave the altar with a clean heart.

Yes, Jesus fed a hungry crowd with just a few fish and a little bread. They were all satisfied, but how few realized what had happened or even took the time to say thank you? When we thank Him in our prayers for all our blessings, is this true thanks or is it lip service we have been taught to give?

If every heart were filled with thanks, there never would be an empty seat at any worship service. We live in a world that God designed and gave to us. Let each of us be truly grateful and give him our praise from our heart, not just from a farce we recite from our memory out of remembrance of what we were taught as children.

Jesus died for each of us on that cross. Let us all be thankful and give Him our deepest praise and thanksgiving.

My Representative

"...and if as my representatives you give a cup of cold water to a little child, you will surely be rewarded."—Matthew 10:42

The other day while I was reading over the Gospel lesson for the coming week, this verse kept coming into my mind. After a while it steeled in my thinking what He was trying to tell us. Whatever we do, we must do it in His name.

We can feed people's hearts, souls, and stomachs. It will not do them or us any good unless we do it as a representative of Jesus. It is Christ who must be behind it. It must be for His glory and not for our own satisfaction.

God does not make deals. He pours His blessing on everyone, but it is up to us to receive these blessings and pass them on to others.

As I was watching the news on television the other night, they showed how people were dying from the lack of drinkable water. This is something that never enters our minds. Just another blessing we receive every day. A few well-placed wells with purification units could save many lives. God has put the water there, but it is left up to man to use the knowledge to make the water drinkable. He has done His part. Will mankind do their part?

Following the water story, they showed pictures of a new type of military machine that had cost over 80 million dollars to make. I thought, *Yes, it will help our soldiers in battle and save some lives. But why can't we live in a world where that money could have been used to develop units to give drinking water to many?*

What have you done lately acting as God's representative? What will it take to motivate us to reach out to others in His name?

New Year's Promise

"And he said unto them, 'Go ye into all the world, and preach the gospel to every creature.' "—Mark 16:15

With a new year comes challenges of living in a world so filled with evil. We must continue to reach out and share the good news of Christ and His death to save all of mankind. We can't just leave it up to the pastors and those who have been trained for the job. We must share our faith with those we meet. It is a fact that the more we share our faith, the stronger it is to us.

We remember that Jesus said we must remove the log from our eye before we try to take the splinter from our brother's eye. Yes, our life must stay in His ways.

Each year most of use make New Year's resolutions, so this year let us resolve that if possible, we will share our faith in Christ with someone each day. Who knows? It could be your witness to His love that will turn someone's life around.

The changing of the evil-filled world has to start somewhere. Why can't it begin with you and me?

During the past year I heard a professor challenge his graduates with a great problem. He asked them to imagine that they were told they had 24 hours to live. He asked them, "Whom would you call to tell this news?" He asked them to make those calls anyway because they should let those people know how much they are cared about.

I would like to urge you to call someone and start your own little drive to change our lives.

With the job of Christmas fresh in our memory and a desire to change our world to a better place to live, let us start each day of the New Year with a prayer of thanks to God for the gift of His son for our salvation.

No Other God

In this sinful world in which we live, we are tempted every day in many ways. It is so important that we remember the rules God gave us when he gave Moses the Ten Commandments.

The first and main one is that there is and can never be but one God. It was God who made the world and rules it always. We are all His creation. He made us and loves us as we are told in our church services. He has made a place for us in His kingdom, but we must claim that place. Jesus taught us, "I am the way. You cannot come to My Father's house except through Me."

Yes, it is our faith in following that Jesus taught us how to do. Once He takes over your life, you have the key to His kingdom. This does not mean you will not be tempted or that you can run wild as did the Prodigal Son. It means—that like the Son—we must come to Jesus asking for forgiveness. Jesus paid the price on the cross.

Throughout recorded history there has been evil on earth that caused people to hurt each other in many different ways. God went to Abraham and told him he would father a great people. Over the ages God has stayed true to this promise.

The same God who led David to be the king of His people has no limits. Through our faith God will lead us to fulfill His mission here and now.

We must remember that God is the same yesterday, today, and tomorrow. His love for us has and always will be the same. He sent His son to assure each of us we are His people. Stop and listen. In His own way, He will guide you, but you must make the choice to listen each and every day.

Peace Be With You

"On the evening of that day, the first day of the week, the doors being shut where the disciples were, for fear of the Jews, Jesus came and stood among them and said to them, 'Peace be with you.' "—John 20:19

Christ's greeting to His disciples after He arose from the tomb was "God's peace be with you." This greeting is still true today for each of us who are His present-day disciples. If we accept Him as our Savior and place our hope in His word, He will grant each of us this perfect peace. It is there and it is our choice. We must totally live by His word, or it will not come to pass.

The power of His peace can and will help in your life, but your faith must be totally in Him with no exceptions, no matter what they might be.

You cannot see it, but you will feel it. Others will see it and can tell by your actions and reactions.

Thomas did not believe that the others had seen Christ until he himself touched His side and hands. After that experience, Thomas also believed and received the peace. Christ told him that he believed because he had seen and felt the wounds but that others would believe by accepting His teachings.

I have not been able to find in the Bible where there is room for doubt. From the fiery furnaces to the march out of Egypt to the cross, all was done through faith in God's word. There was never any room for doubt.

This still rings true today. Unless we trust in His word, we will not receive His perfect peace.

May God's peace bless each of our lives.

Peace Granted For Us

"May the Lord show you his favor and give you his peace."
—Numbers 6:26

Each time we go to the altar for communion, we pray for God's peace in our lives. In that quiet time at the altar, we seem to experience that peace. But when we return to our pews, do we lose that feeling? What happens when our thoughts turn from God and back to the hectic world we live in? Somehow we must learn to leave our problems with Him as He has told us to do. God called us and as church members, we have accepted this call.

Put your trust in Him and through faith give Him the things that disturb your peace. Each time I read the Old Testament I can see what a problem He had getting the people to stay within His guidelines. The people were taken as slaves to Egypt and they prayed to God for freedom. So—using Moses—He led them out of slavery. But they still were not happy and at times prayed to go back to Egypt. They were never content, because they never put their full faith in God's love.

Like the people of the Old Testament, we must listen to God's words and obey him. Nothing should come before our faith in Him. Like the people of old, we should be careful what we ask for.

Samuel's mother was childless for years, and she prayed and prayed, promising to give her child to the service of the church. When Samuel was born, she lived up to her word and it hurt her. But as soon as possible, she gave him to the church to begin his life serving the Lord. Later on, she was blessed with many more children to fill her life, so her prayers were answered. It was because of her faith in giving up Samuel in order to keep her promise to God that He gave her the thing she wanted.

Put your faith in God and He will grant the peace you ask for.

The End of Time
Revelations 20:1-15

In a recent Bible-study class, we went through the book of Revelations, which seemed to me like it was written in some kind of code. Based on the information given in Revelations, many people have tried to figure out when the end of time will come. Many disasters that are to face the believers are mentioned. But in the end, good will overcome evil and all will live in a new world in the presence of God.

In Revelations 20, verses 12 and 15, it says that each person is recorded in the *Book of Life*. There is no mention of what is written there, but it does say that from what is there, it will be determined whether or not the person will spend eternity in the new world with God.

This got me thinking about what was on my page. *Was it good or evil? Did the good things I have done outnumber the bad?*

The author of the study book cited many verses from the Old and New Testaments that foretell the coming of the Day of Judgment and the coming of the new world, but no one knows when it will be. Our only hope is to live each day as if it were the last and to trust our Savior to be with us on that day.

God is perfect and everything that He has created is perfect, but mankind has made it evil. The author summed it up best by saying God's favorable judgment is an expression of grace.

Let us all live so that when the time comes that we are to stand trial for being a Christian, there will be enough evidence to convict us.

The Meaning of Faith

"Now faith is the assurance of things hoped for, the conviction of things not seen. Indeed, by faith our ancestors received approval. By faith we understand that the worlds were prepared by the word of God, so that what is seen was made from things that are not visible."—Hebrews 11:1-3

A few weeks ago our pastor spoke to us about fear. He mentioned in his talk with the children how many people fear snakes, bugs, and all kinds of things. In his sermon to the adults, he mentioned the fears of death, change, and many other things.

It got me thinking about my fears and how some of them have changed. I did fear storms, but after going through a hurricane on a warship in the North Atlantic, that fear went away. As a child, I had an awful fear of death, but with age and my faith in Jesus, I have overcome that as well. My greatest fear was tithing to the church. For years, as a family, we had supported the church with both time and money. One year my wife and I decided it was time for us to start to tithe and give our ten percent. But how could we? We had three children, a home mortgage, a car payment, and other debts to pay. After much prayer and talking, on that Commitment Sunday, we signed up to give ten percent of our income to our church. By doing that we knew we were putting our whole future in the hands of our Lord. We both had doubts, but our faith was so strong we knew He would not steer us wrong. We always tried to write the church check first and somehow everything else got paid.

I think that when I overcame that fear, I realized that anything is possible if only we trust in God.

Another example of this faith is what has been happening recently here at our own church. The council saw the need for work on the building and—acting on faith—moved ahead to meet those needs. The response of the congregation has been amazing, both in work done by members and in the money given to support it.

All things are possible through faith. We all should remember that our faith is the only thing that can't be taken away from us. Each day we face someone or something that is trying to take our health, wealth, and freedom. But as long as our faith remains strong in our Savior and His promises, He will show us the way.

Trust and Love

"For God so loved the world that He gave His only son, that whoever believes in Him should not perish but have eternal life."
—John 3:16

With the passing of Christmas and the starting of a new year, we should reflect on just what this means to us. Of all the gifts ever given, this must be the most important and greatest because it was given to all mankind. It was a gift of love and concern given to everyone who will accept it. A gift of hope for the future of all.

For years, at most major sports events or other places where large crowds gathered, someone would hold up a sign to remind us of this gift. As the years have passed, prayer and other religious acts have slowly disappeared. When was the last time you noticed this? Let us all accept this gift that God has given us. Let's all take it and put it to work. Something given in love should be shared in love, not put on a shelf to be used later.

Share what you have been given with those you meet each day. You never know what it may mean to others because the more you give it away, the more it will mean to you.

God gave His son to die for our sins. All He asks for in return is our trust and love.

Yes, it was a gift. We did not earn it. All we have to do is accept it.

What Do You Use For Bait?

"And he said to them, 'Follow me, and I will make you fishers of men.' "—Matthew 4:19

As far back as I can remember reading the Bible, Jesus called His followers to be fishers of men. He used the talent that God had given Him and had very few who did not heed His call. Those who became His followers dedicated their lives to the spreading of His kingdom.

When we accepted His call, we too became fishers of men. It is our duty to help bring people into the fold. This task gets harder each day with all the things that are vying for every minute of our time.

Some churches are changing their music and their way of preaching. And they are going out in buses to bring people to church. But this will not keep the people there. We must become mirrors and reflect the love we receive from God back to others. We cannot be like a sponge and just soak up the love for our own use. If we do, we will soon bog down in our own self-love.

Christian love is an amazing thing. The more we share it with others, the more it means to us. So the next time you go fishing for new people to worship our God, be sure to bait the hook with a large piece of love. That is the answer. If others can see what your faith means to you, they will come seeking the same love to help them down life's busy trail.

Cast our faith out to others and watch how our nets fill up in return.

About the Author

James Delar Cox was born November 5, 1925, at home in Stone Mountain, Georgia. He graduated from high school in 1943 and served in the U.S. Navy from November 1, 1944, until February 6, 1946.

He married Ethel Blackwell on July 14, 1946. They had one son, James A., and two daughters: Carollyn G. Barlow and Donna L. Thompson. After Ethel went to the Lord, Jimmy married Shirley M. Matthews on November 10, 1986.

Jimmy loves to write poems when inspired by God. He also loves to bake and share with friends. Today he still makes cakes and pies for special occasions.

www.ingramcontent.com/pod-product-compliance
Lightning Source LLC
Chambersburg PA
CBHW050557170426
43201CB00011B/1730